S0-BDL-511

Dancing with Gogos
A Peace Corps Memoir

Gary P. Cornelius

A PEACE CORPS WRITERS BOOK

Dancing With Gogos
A Peace Corps Memoir

A Peace Corps Writers Book
An imprint of Peace Corps Worldwide

Copyright © 2014 by Gary P. Cornelius
All rights reserved.

Printed in the United States of America
by Peace Corps Writers of Oakland, California.

No part of this book may be used or reproduced in any manner
whatsoever without written permission except in the case of brief
quotations contained in critical articles or reviews. For more
information, contact peacecorpsworldwide@gmail.com.

Peace Corps Writers and the Peace Corps Writers colophon are
trademarks of PeaceCorpsWorldwide.org.

ISBN 978-1-935925-50-7
Library of Congress Control Number: 2014945375

First Peace Corps Writers Edition, July 2014

"…the time has come to return home, and although I do not know if my feet will ever again touch the red soil of the land I've grown to love so well, Africa will remain a part of me as I leave an aged piece of my heart behind in the place that taught me more about humanity in two years than I'd learned in a lifetime."

Alyssa Bonini, Peace Corps Volunteer
3/9/14, upon departure from Africa

Table of Contents

Acknowledgements

Dancing with Gogos is the story of my efforts to make a difference in a collection of Zulu villages in rural South Africa, while fulfilling my lifelong dream of being a Peace Corps volunteer. That dream dates to 1970 when I was fifteen, not many years after Peace Corps was created by President John F. Kennedy in 1961.

I would like to acknowledge the support of my family, especially my daughter, Megan MacCullen, who unfailingly supported and encouraged me to pursue my dream, even when we learned I would be going to a country with one of the highest crime rates in the world. Her family also kept my beloved eleven-year-old dog, Carly (now fourteen), while I was away, making their family her family.

I would like to acknowledge my thirty-five fellow volunteers in SA25, the twenty-fifth group of volunteers to train and serve in the Republic of South Africa since the first group arrived in 1997 after a meeting between President Bill Clinton and President Nelson Mandela. Not all of us made it to the end, but oh what a ride, eh? It was an honor and a privilege to serve with you—most of you in your mid-twenties—and I wish glorious futures for all. I would also like to recognize the dedicated and hard-working Peace Corps South Africa staff at "post." Many were the times we received emails from HQ that came well after 5 p.m. A special shout out to Training Manager Victor Baker, keeper of the sanctity, and the proper singing of, the South African national anthem.

Thanks also to those who read parts or all of my manuscript, providing valuable feedback so it would be the best book possible. They include John Kanelis, Dave Peters, John Reed of writerswelcome.com, Megan MacCullen and Jeanne Marie Moore. And thanks, again, to my talented daughter Megan for the great cover design, and to my Peace Corps volunteer colleague Cara Drinovsky for the cover photo of me holding the hand of five-year-old Siyabonga, with whom I lived during training in the village of Bundu.

My biggest thanks go to the many rural South Africans who opened their hearts, their lives and many their homes and families to me—for teaching me about your culture, your language, your way of life, your sorrows and travails, and your dreams…especially, The Bhuta Family in Bundu, the Zungu Family in Goodhome, Nonhlanhla Radebe, my supervisor, and all her family, Mdu and Amanda and their family…and to Sindisiwe, a Zulu woman.

Gary Cornelius, Eugene, OR, USA/June 2014

1

Leaving the Village

I walked through the door of my small pink cinderblock house about 6:15 a.m., as I had done nearly every morning for a year. As usual, the sun was rising to my left, but, equally striking, a full moon graced the west, about to drop behind The Drakensburg, an African mountain range about twenty-five kilometers from where I lived. Over those mountains: the landlocked country of Lesotho. In front of me—the view marred only by an outhouse, sixty feet away—sat Ntabamhlophe (en-ta-bom-SHLO-pay), which means White Mountain in isi-Zulu, the language of the Zulu people. It's a large, flat-topped mesa, not unlike those seen all over the western United States and over much of South Africa. I'd never lived so close to one, being a city boy growing up in Portland, Oregon. I never tired of enjoying the mountain's beauty and had photographed it many times from various angles, posting pictures on Facebook and ever-fattening the photo file from my African experience.

I had vowed to my friend Mdu, who had lived there his whole life, that I would one day let him guide me to the top, a long hike. A trip that offered not only the prospect of a grand view in all directions, but a chance we might encounter a mamba or a spitting cobra, not generally seen in villages, where people kill them, but not uncommon in "the bush" that surrounded the mountain. Two of the most potentially dangerous snakes in Africa. Our hike would be on a Sunday, or holiday, since Mdu worked fulltime at the Imbabazane Municipal Library, Monday through Saturday. (Imbabazane is an African tree common in the area). Alas, the hike was not to be.

March 27, 2013: Not yet my last official day as a United States Peace Corps volunteer. I was leaving the village in an hour—to be escorted by Silence, a Peace Corps driver, back to Pretoria, for my thirty-hour trip to the U.S. It was, in all likelihood, the last time I would see this view and the beautiful rural country on the drive north. It reminded me of the rolling hills of Eastern Oregon. I stood in the dirt in front of my door for several minutes, taking it all in, trying to memorize it so that I would never forget. The colors—the mountain covered by beautiful green foliage, not yet burned by the villagers in an annual ritual, the orange and pink rays of the sun, the green metal roofs of nearby houses and the yurt-like rondavels, with roofs of dried grass. I needed to remember the smells—dirt, damp from morning dew, the trash barrel, the family peach trees; cow pies, goat droppings and chicken shit; the sounds—crowing roosters, chickens scratching for bugs, bleating goats on the dirt road on their way to graze for the day; the distinctive sound of a cow bell swinging up the road; singing birds.

No people. It was too early for the hundreds of children who would be marching to school in their matching brown and gold uniforms, swinging book bags or sporting backpacks, dodging mud puddles, the boys kicking homemade soccer balls fashioned from dozens of plastic bread bags, stuffed together and tied off with a knot. Adults who needed to get to town for work had already taken a village taxi to the city of Estcourt, traveling along a narrow, bumpy dirt road which intersected with a larger dirt road about three hundred meters up a grade. Being at the bottom of that grade had interfered with my cell phone reception many times, cutting off straight-line access to the nearest cell phone tower.

I was alone. Mr. Zungu, the patriarch of the family compound where I lived with about six other people—a shifting number of his nieces and nephews—had already left for his sixty-kilometer commute to Bergville, a small city to the north where he was principal of a high school. No one else was up yet. He would not be home for at least twelve hours, and I would be long gone, boarding a plane in Johannesburg about the same time he would honk for someone inside the house to open the gate for his black pick-up, his "bakkie." Occasionally, that had been me when no one else was around.

My departure from the village of Goodhome, a year earlier than planned, was necessitated by my recent diagnosis of Parkinson's disease, a disorder easily treated in the U.S., and made well known by actor Michael J. Fox, who was diagnosed at age thirty-five. But in a remote Zulu village in rural South Africa? Not so much, the Peace Corps medical staff in Washington had decided. I disagreed. My research suggested my symptoms would progress slowly over many years. But it didn't matter what I thought. I was to be "medevacced" to my "home of record," Eugene, Oregon, for further evaluation and treatment. It didn't look like I would be returning. If the diagnosis held, I would be "medically separated" or "med-sepped" as we say in Peace Corps lingo. There was a small chance they would decide my condition could be treated in Africa, or that a second opinion would find something different, and I would return to Africa to finish my two-year, nine-week commitment to Peace Corps. But it was not to be. The diagnosis held and I stayed in the U.S.

2

The Forty-year Wait

I told my story countless times in the nearly two years before I left for Africa, first to friends and relatives, later at my orientation in Philadelphia, during training and, eventually, to rural African villagers: the story began in 1970, at the age of fifteen, when I decided I wanted to join Peace Corps, the volunteer organization started by President Kennedy in 1961 to help in developing countries. As I write these words in June 2013, more than 8,000 volunteers are in about seventy countries. At one time or another Peace Corps has been in 139 countries and more than 215,000 people have volunteered.

But I didn't make it early on. I grew up, went to college, had a career, had a child and got married. Thoughts of Peace Corps service went on the back burner. For more than forty years. Then one day I realized that since I'd worked in Oregon's public mental health and developmental disabilities systems twenty-eight years. I could retire early at fifty-five and get a modest pension. I could have worked a few more years and made more money, but I didn't want more money. I wanted more time to do things I'd always wanted to do, like travel and join Peace Corps. And, as if I needed to further rationalize retiring early, it would mean that someone else at the county wouldn't get laid off. Probably someone who needed that job more than I did.

My daughter was grown, and a long relationship had ended abruptly, unexpectedly and painfully. Even without motivation provided by Peace Corps, moving to Africa seemed like a grand idea. No one ever topped my story about the forty-year wait to join, though a couple of people came close. Vivian, a seventy-eight-year-old African-American great-grandmother from Austin, Texas who used to work for the Veterans Administration, was older than Miss Lillian, President Jimmy Carter's mother, who was in her early seventies when she went to India to be a Peace Corps volunteer in the 1960s. When I left Africa Vivian invited me to visit and accompany her to a tailgater in honor of her grandson, who had been a starter for the Louisiana State University football team. In an article by Mark Miller of Reuters News Service that was published as my training group was wrapping up its two-year term, and not long after Vivian's eightieth birthday, Miller described her as, "The oldest person to serve since the Peace Corps was signed into existence in 1961 by President John F. Kennedy." And I got to train and serve with her!

The forty-year wait almost became permanent. I learned early on that the average length of time from the date you submit your application to the day you leave for training is about fourteen months. It was nineteen months for me because my medical history meant that I was formally rejected, twice, for medical reasons. But I appealed the decision. I argued and negotiated with the Peace Corps medical screeners in Washington, D.C. and when, finally, my urologist in Eugene wrote a letter on my behalf that made the difference, I had flowers delivered to his office to show my gratitude.

The problem was that in the mid-'90s I had bladder cancer, an unusual cancer for someone who had never smoked. It was caught early and treated successfully. But it's a cancer that tends to recur, so for years I've had an annual cystoscopy, to ensure that no cancer has returned. A "cysto" is an intrusive procedure that involves a long tube, with a camera on the end, being inserted into a very private place to see if new tumors are growing. Over the years I became quite the seasoned veteran of the procedure. Over time the technology improved, the tube became flexible plastic instead of metal, and I went from being medicated with a fast-acting, memory-inhibiting and effective drug, Versed, that knocked me out, to staying awake and chatting with the urologist while he did his work. I had the added benefit of being able to observe the monitor and watch the whole thing.

My first urologist retired a couple of years after I started seeing him and I was assigned to a different physician. I saw him for two years before he died of cancer. The practice gave me a list of the remaining half-dozen or so doctors and told me to pick one. Completely at random, I chose Dr. Thomas Kollmorgen because I thought he had an interesting name. He's been my urology guy ever since. Ironically, that history of cancer made my blood unacceptable when I tried to donate blood in Africa, even though I had donated a hundred times in the U.S. I was also at high risk for prostate cancer because my father had died of it in 2001, but that didn't seem to concern the Peace Corps medical people, perhaps because it's a slow-growing cancer. They say that every man would die of prostate cancer if he didn't die of something else first.

I had been cancer-free for more than fifteen years, but the Peace Corps medical people in D.C., as well as those in the South African Blood Services, were not impressed. After reviewing my records, Peace Corps sent me a letter saying that a cystoscopy might be a routine procedure in Eugene, Oregon, but not so in a developing country. I was rejected. The letter said I could appeal, but that there was no point unless I had "new information." I completed the appeal form and included a plan for dealing with my annual need for the exam—new information. I proposed that I take complete responsibility for my cystoscopy: I would arrange it, pay for it, do it on my own time, not Peace Corps time, come home or travel to another country, if necessary, at my own expense.

Along the way I tried to enlist the support of Jeff Merkley, one of Oregon's two United States senators. I wrote to the senator, included an explanation of the issue and a copy of the plan I had developed, and sent it off. I asked for his agreement that the plan I had developed was a reasonable response to Peace Corps concerns. A couple of weeks went by and I got a call from one of the senator's aides, who said she was sorry, but that the senator's policy was to not write letters of recommendation for people he did not personally know. "For all we know, you may have murdered your last wife," she told me. I wanted to tell her that, actually, my last wife murdered me—metaphorically speaking, anyway. But I didn't. Nor did I point out that I wasn't asking for a reference, I was asking for the senator's agreement that the plan I presented was reasonable. But the senator's office didn't see that distinction. It was a dead end. (A few months later I got a nice card from the senator, congratulating me on my recent swearing in as a volunteer).

Another couple of weeks went by and I had a call from Elizabeth, the Peace Corps nurse who was shepherding my records through the onerous medical review process. We had talked before by phone, exchanged letters and emails. She was always professional, sympathetic and thoughtful. I had begun to think I should start calling her "Liz." From her voice I guessed she was African American, mid- to late thirties. Referring to my proposal to take responsibility for the annual cysto, Elizabeth said that Peace Corps was responsible for the medical care of all volunteers and wasn't willing to delegate any of it to someone else – including me and my urologist in Eugene or anywhere else I might choose to have the procedure done. There was a long pause while I digested this information. *"I guess that's it…I won't be traveling to a foreign country for Peace Corps,"* I thought. *"Rejected again."* But the conversation wasn't over.

"But," Elizabeth said, pausing for dramatic effect, "If you can get your doctor in Eugene to write a letter saying you can skip that procedure for one year…we'll take you." I was back in business. I'd have the procedure done before I left, when I returned, and skip the one year in the middle. I wrote Dr. K a letter explaining what I needed and why. I didn't have a lot of confidence he would agree with the proposal, but it was my last and only hope. I was in for a surprise. He said that the longer one goes without having a recurrence of bladder cancer, the greater the chance that you won't get it again. He was fine with skipping a year. He wrote the letter and I was accepted.

I still had dental records to submit, but as long as the dentist didn't find anything that couldn't be fixed, that wouldn't be a problem. This was the second complete set of dental records, exams and x-rays I was submitting. They are only good for one year and the process had taken so long that the first records I submitted—at my own expense of $300, since I no longer had dental insurance—had expired by a couple of weeks. I had to pay another $300 for a new exam and an updated set of records. They passed muster and shortly I got the long-awaited letter, congratulating me on my appointment to be an "HIV Outreach Worker," in Peace Corps South Africa's Community HIV/AIDS Outreach

Program, or CHOP. I was now a "nominee," in Peace Corps lingo, and would be until I arrived at training camp. Not until we had successfully completed nine weeks of training and been sworn in—taking the same oath as U.S. Marines, CIA agents and Foreign Service officers—would I and my thirty-five fellow trainees actually become volunteers. I was especially gratified when I learned that only thirty-six percent of applicants are eventually offered assignments.

Peace Corps had allowed me in my application to indicate the region where I wanted to be placed, though there are never guarantees. I requested Northern Africa, thinking that it would be interesting to live in Morocco or Tunisia for two years. This was before the "Arab Spring" phenomenon that resulted in fighting for democracy in those and other countries. My second choice was Central America, a place I've traveled to a couple of times and in which I'd always had an interest. And I speak enough Spanish to get by when I travel there. A couple of months went by and I got a call from the Peace Corps recruiter in Seattle who had interviewed me in Eugene. She told me Peace Corps probably would not send me to Northern Africa because I didn't speak French. Those are former French colonies and proficiency in that language is valued in volunteers sent there. "But we'll send you somewhere else in Africa, sub-Saharan Africa," she said.

Peace Corps also told me in my appointment letter why they were sending me to South Africa. They had learned from my medical records that I had talked to a counselor after the end of my long relationship. They were only willing to place me in a country where psychiatric medications were readily available, "in case you have a relapse and need antidepressants." Later, ironically, I would become a member of the Peace Corps South Africa Volunteer Support Network, a group who counseled and supported new and at times veteran volunteers who were struggling. Many were younger people far away from home for the first time, or who became homesick later, or had problems in their villages—disillusionment, sexual harassment, trouble with colleagues, or dealing with family or personal issues back home from a remote African village.

Some of my most interesting experiences were a result of being a part of the VSN. But, just as when I worked in Oregon's public mental health system, I was sworn to maintain confidentiality of my interactions with volunteers or trainees, so I can't mention those most interesting experiences. When I got home in the spring of 2013, a year early, Peace Corps offered to send me to a psychiatrist or other mental health professional for counseling or medication. I laughed and told the "international health care coordinator," "Thanks, but I have a hundred friends who are counseling professionals who will talk to me, listen to me and support me—for free. Save your money."

Months before our departures, I and other nominees from the Eugene area, headed for other countries, would be recognized at the annual "nom party" organized by West Cascade Peace Corps Association. West Cascade is an active organization of returned Peace Corps volunteers from the southern Willamette Valley in western Oregon. There are similar organizations all over the world. West Cascade supports would-be volunteers, promotes Peace Corps at local festivals and events, and raises money for projects of Oregon volunteers in their countries of service. I had been attending their potlucks for more than a year and often wore a tee-shirt I bought at a fund-raising event. It read, "We Must Be the Change We Want to See in The World," a statement attributed to Mahatma Gandhi. Eugene's mayor at the time, Kitty Piercy, and her husband, David, were Peace Corps volunteers in the 1960s—she in Ethiopia and he in Iran—and met during their service. A few months after I returned I was elected to West Cascade's board of directors.

Volunteers in education were known as the School and Community Resource Project. They were teachers. But the job of CHOP, the health program, was to aid in the fight against the HIV/AIDS epidemic that makes South Africa one of the highest rated countries in the world. Our placements and assignments in villages over three provinces would reflect that. The two hundred Peace Corps volunteers in South Africa are roughly split between the two programs.

I became part of "SA25," the twenty-fifth group of trainees to enter the Republic of South Africa since 1997, not long after President Bill Clinton met with Nelson Mandela and suggested the United States could help the fledgling democracy by sending Peace Corps volunteers to help with the AIDS crisis.

There were thirty-six in my group or "cohort," as we say in Peace Corps—thirty women and six men—two married couples, from Seattle, and two women who were married but whose husbands were not with them. Most of the thirty women were in their early to mid-twenties, roughly in line with the average Peace Corps volunteer being female and about twenty-eight. Eight of us—about twenty-two percent—were over age fifty; worldwide, about eight percent of active volunteers are older. Apparently I wasn't the only over-fifty volunteer sent to the country with a better medical system than other African nations. Until we all met in Philadelphia for staging and orientation in January 2012, I wondered if I might be the oldest. But in addition to seventy-eight-year-old Vivian, there was Peggie, in her sixties, from Southern California, Linda and Susan, whose husbands hadn't joined us, and Greg and Pat, one of the married couples. (The other married couple, Christopher and Emily, was in their mid-twenties). All the other fifty-plussers were older than me. Linda, a nurse and former hospital administrator from Bend, Oregon, became one of my best Peace Corps friends. Susan was from Virginia and was not to be confused with Ohioan "Doc Susan," a retired cardiologist. She also was over fifty but wouldn't tell me her age for the longest time. The third Oregonian in the group was twenty-two-ish Alyssa, recently out of college, from Portland. I calculated that three Oregonians of thirty-six was better than eight percent of the total, even though Oregon has only about one percent of the population of the United States. So our state was well represented. In fact, in 2013 Oregon ranked fourth per capita—behind only Vermont, New Hampshire and The District of Columbia—in the number of Peace Corps volunteers produced. The University of Oregon has a perennial spot in the top ten college producers of volunteers. And in a quirk of fate that could make one believe in the "six degrees of separation" theory, Alyssa and I, though we had never met before, learned we had a mutual friend in Portland. That friend had gone to grad school with John Jacoby, the Peace Corps country director for South Africa whom we were about to meet after our sixteen-hour flight from JFK International in New York to Johannesburg. But first: orientation.

3

Orientation

I was one of the last to arrive in Philly that night, having flown cross country from Eugene, further than most, to make my way to the hotel where we would be until departure for Africa in thirty-six hours. My roommate was the same person I would share a room with once we arrived in South Africa, but before we had been assigned to our host families.

Donovan, a twenty-five-year-old from Los Angeles was the product of an African-American father and a white mother. Light-skinned but with the curly hair characteristic of many African Americans, he was good looking, delightful, funny, personable, humble, intelligent, good at learning language, and adored by young African girls. I liked him immediately. A couple of months later several of us were talking about finding romance in Africa. Donovan said, without any hint of bravado or arrogance, "I don't chase girls, girls chase me." He wasn't even smiling, merely stating a fact. He was right. Eventually, he was appointed as one of three trainee leaders who met weekly with the training manager to represent the rest of us in issues such as training information, or in regard to planning events. Donovan had been teaching English in South Korea before he left to accept his Peace Corps assignment. Sadly, he "ET'd"—early termination—a few months before I did.

That first night several of us gathered in the lobby and decided to walk to a nearby restaurant for dinner. Most of our group, me included, ordered alcohol, living up to the reputation of Peace Corps volunteers worldwide as people who like to drink and have a good time. That would turn out to be a problem for some of the younger volunteers, despite the matter being addressed, more than once, in training. We introduced ourselves, and told where we came from. That might have been the first time I met Linda and Alyssa, my fellow Oregonians, though we had communicated earlier via a Facebook discussion group dedicated to SA25, started by Christopher, the computer geek from Seattle who had worked at a Mac store. The same Christopher who taught me the meaning of the word "bomb" as an adjective to describe something, like a band. In the '50s it was "cool," in the '60s "groovy," and in the '70s "radical." I don't know what it was in the '80s and the '90s. The first part of the '80s I was living in Alaska, where everything is always cool, especially outside, and the next twenty years were the most stressful of my mental health career and I didn't have time or energy to think about groovy adjectives. A lot of the twenty-somethings used the bomb word.

Peace Corps sent me an abundance of information about South Africa to review before heading for Philly, some of which we would discuss as orientation continued. The three largest land mammals in Africa—elephants, hippos and rhinos—and the tallest, giraffes, roam in the wild—well, in large, fenced preserves and national parks, some bigger than Rhode Island. Some of the deadliest snakes on the planet also live there. Snakes with names like puff adder, black mamba (average length: eight feet), boomslang and spitting cobra. South Africa is larger than California and Texas combined, has deserts, mountains, oceans, jungles, plateaus, savannah, forests and everything in between. Imagine a crop grown anywhere in the world, Peace Corps said, and it can probably be grown there: South Africa, my home for the next twenty-six-plus months.

We all went to bed pretty late that night and I suspect many of us were, like me, a bit too excited to sleep. I found a computer terminal where I could check email and post a short note on Facebook for my friends and relatives back home, along with a warning that I had no idea what the next few weeks held, what my Internet access would be, or when I would be in contact again.

The next morning came early and after a quick breakfast we gathered in a large meeting room in the basement of the hotel. Lots of paper work ensued after meeting Patrick, the "country desk officer" for South Africa at Peace Corps headquarters in Washington. He told us what we would experience in the coming weeks and months, but the story I remember most vividly was the one he told about Miss Lillian, President Carter's mother. Patrick said that many years after she had returned from service in India and had passed away, a U.S. government official was at a meeting in India with Indian leaders, including a woman who had been a young girl when she met Miss Lillian and was influenced by her. The woman, now a government official, was trying to make her country a better place. She attributed her rise from poor, remote villager to a leader in her country to the influence of the president's mother. An influence Miss Lillian probably never knew. (In 1998, Miss Lillian's great-grandson, Jason Carter, President Carter's grandson, would follow her legacy and become a Peace Corps volunteer in South Africa in one of the first groups to enter the country lead by Nelson Mandela).

Patrick told us this story as an example of how the influence of one's Peace Corps service might not be apparent for many years, and the person who caused the influence might not ever be aware of it. I thought about that story often during my service, on days when I questioned whether I was having an impact. Toward the end of SA25's service my fellow Oregonian, Alyssa, wrote in her blog: "When you do outreach work in a community for two years, *any* kind of confirmation that your work means something to somebody else is a blessing that will make your day for weeks and weeks afterward." It's a sentiment to which I and likely all Peace Corps volunteers could relate.

I liked Patrick's story because I have long been an admirer of President Carter, especially his work in founding the Carter Center in Atlanta, Georgia to pursue peace and democracy in developing countries. Though he became what is commonly described as "the leader of the free world," I think his most important work came after he left office. Twice in my younger days I wrote what I thought were impressive letters of application and sent them off to the Carter Center, along with a resume, and asked for any low-level job. I wasn't hired, but got very nice rejection letters from the chief of staff. My opportunity for world travel to pursue development work in places where it was needed had to wait for a couple more decades, since my effort, eight times, to become a foreign service officer at the State Department also failed.

After much paperwork and Patrick's story we introduced ourselves, told where we were from, and something we had learned about South Africa. I shared that I had learned that South Africa was home of the black mamba, one of the deadliest snakes in the world, growing to eight to ten feet in length, and capable of moving at the rate of five meters per second, "the length of my full-sized pickup back in Oregon," I told the group. A returned Peace Corps volunteer back in Eugene once told me that the only thing she didn't like about her experience in Cameroon was "sharing the dirt road with eight-foot long black mambas when I had to teach a night class."

After that story some people assumed, incorrectly, that I was afraid of snakes and teased me about it. Actually, I have a healthy respect for snakes, especially venomous ones, and while it's true I hate to be surprised by a snake while on a hiking trail (who doesn't) I'm not obsessively fearful of them. Once, hiking in sage brush in eastern Montana, I nearly stepped on a six-foot rattlesnake as big around as the fattest part of my arm, and the same color as the sage brush. But the snake's warning system worked like it was supposed to and I retreated when I was one step from being within striking distance. Not long after I arrived in South Africa I joined a Facebook discussion group, "Snakes of South Africa," that provided hours of entertainment, reading about members' interactions with various snakes, many of whose pictures were posted. I learned that there is a countrywide network of skilled, amateur, snake handlers/herpetologists, who, on their own nickel, are willing to be called out on short notice to capture and relocate snakes, rather than see them killed. The nest of baby cobras found during our training, not far from where we slept, weren't so lucky. One of our South African language instructors reportedly dispatched them with a shovel. Valentine's Day came just a couple of weeks into training and we had the opportunity to share sentiments. Lilly gave me a valentine—a piece of paper torn into the shape of Oregon—that read "I will step in front of every black mamba for you!" Fortunately, she never had to keep that promise.

The meeting in the hotel basement was the first opportunity for us all to compare notes and start assessing the personalities, the skills, of our new training mates. In the afternoon we broke into groups and engaged in various exercises, and "ice breakers," to see how fast we could think on our feet, show leadership skills, solve problems, engage in teamwork, communicate without talking, and get along with others. Such exercises, we would learn, are a hallmark of Peace Corps and we would do many of them in the coming weeks in pre-service training, PST, once we arrived in Africa. One such group exercise would enable me to proposition five gorgeous women for unprotected sex.

We learned that day that Ohio also was well represented in our group. I don't recall exactly how many Ohioans there were, but I think more than from any other state. Cindy, the only one of our group who was in her forties, was from Ohio. Washington State had about the same number. The Ohioans included one of the two Susans, the cardiologist. Only one of us, Emily Gill from Auburn, Alabama, was from the Deep South. Emily, a music major who also had worked with people who experience disabilities, was also the only SA25er who brought a musical instrument, her guitar. And she could sing! She was not to be confused with Emily Gerth-Guyette, who was the other half of the young married couple from Seattle. That Emily was married to Christopher Kemp, but, because they had different last names, though married, sometimes they were assigned to separate rooms or otherwise separated, a gaffe that went on for months. They married specifically because Peace Corps doesn't allow partnered couples to serve together—only married couples. They rushed their wedding to meet a Peace Corps deadline.

There were a couple of us from Texas, and, one of our youngest, at twenty, was a yoga instructor from Maine. Three of us, including one of the single men, Dan, called the Chicago area home. Dan had been a reporter and early on took an interest in my background as a writer and author of a book. He insisted on buying a copy of my novel, based loosely on my career in mental health, because he wanted to support a fellow writer.

Dan was quiet, but funny, thoughtful and intelligent and had also worked as a community organizer of sorts in Chicago, a history that bears a resemblance to that of another community organizer from Chicago, Barack Obama. Dan's Peace Corps assignment in northern KwaZulu-Natal Province, organizing information and support about the fight against AIDS, reflected his background in Chicago. While waiting for our plane in New York, he had told a funny story. When he was thirteen years old and accompanying a friend and the friend's mother the airport security people found a package of condoms in his carry-on luggage, in front of his friend's mother. And I can't forget Stephanie, a twin from Salt Lake City, who had been a hockey player. She lived near Dan in northern KZN and joined a women's rugby team. She probably still has scars to show for it. And more than once she scored drinks for us by doing fancy card tricks for bartenders.

Ashley, also from the Chicago area, was the only one of us who didn't bring a laptop. The written information Peace Corps had sent us with our acceptance letters said a computer wasn't necessary, but once we were there we learned that email was the main form of communication between post and volunteers in remote villages. Admin expected us to submit various reports and requests via email—including the obnoxious, quarterly "volunteer reporting form," usually shortened to "VRF," on which we were to report our activities. I guess Washington and Pretoria weren't always on the same page. I never did successfully get the VRF to download to my laptop. It wasn't long before Ashley had ordered a laptop from back home. A pink one, as I recall.

Some of the group were openly gay or lesbian, including talkative and outgoing Brant, from Washington, D.C., who left at the end of training to return to the states. That left just me, Donovan and Dan as the only single males in the group. One of our thirty-six would, eventually, come "out of the closet." I've always felt that it spoke well of our cohesion, comfort with one another, our embracing of diversity and level of trust, and our supporting natures that that person was comfortable enough to share such thoughts with the rest of us.

We had four African Americans, including Andrea, a nurse from New Jersey who was born and had lived on the Caribbean island of Trinidad until she was eight years old. The other was Ragan from Chicago—funny and outgoing—the aforementioned Donovan, and Vivian, our senior member, from Texas. We also had a couple of women of Asian heritage, Wilda and Ann, both from Southern California. Ann, like Andrea, had emigrated from another country, Sri Lanka, at an early age. Theresa, from Phoenix, was born in the U.S. but had Iraqi parents who immigrated not long before Saddam Hussein came to power. We were quite a diverse group, and proud of it, and several of us—though not including me—took active roles in organizing and contributing to a Facebook discussion group known by the mouthful Peace Corps South Africa Lesbian, Gay, Bisexual, Transgender, Queer and Ally Volunteers. I became an ally, as did many of the rest of our group.

Among those who helped start this FB group was fellow, now former, Eugene resident Sean Smith, a member of SA23, whom I met during PST when the Peace Corps South Africa Diversity Committee gathered to talk about its work. Sean, in his late forties, was a journalist who left his job as a reporter for Entertainment Weekly (he also worked previously at Newsweek) to become a Peace Corps volunteer. He was funny and personable and often regaled us with tales of interviewing celebrities such as Jodie Foster and Angelina Jolie. He and I spent much time together at Khayalethu, everyone's favorite Pretoria backpacker (hostel), at the end of my service, which coincided with his. He was waiting to "COS" (close of service) and I was waiting to be "med-sepped." He invited me to accompany him on a shopping sortie one day, but I opted for a movie at the local mall. Shopping would have been more fun.

Another speaker from the diversity committee, Doug, who was of Asian descent, spoke about the danger of stereotyping others based on their racial heritage. He told the story of intervening in a fight during a soccer game in his village, and no one was hitting him. Later he learned this was because, "Everyone assumed I knew kung fu because I was Chinese." He didn't!

I would learn eventually that many of SA25's members had studied abroad and had volunteered in foreign countries—Julie had gone to school in Ghana and had contracted malaria in her young life—and traveled internationally for many reasons. All, like me, were idealistic and wanted to make a difference. I learned I had competition when it came to exhibiting leadership. Though I've always been seen as quiet, low-key and easy going, I've also always been viewed as the person in a group willing to step forward, take charge, do the right thing and get the job done. *I'm now in a group of 36 where most are the same way. No shortage of leaders here,"* I wrote in my journal not long after training started.

At the end of that first day we learned we would be departing the hotel about one o'clock the next morning for the two-hour bus drive from Philly to JFK. The logistics of such a move were challenging and Patrick asked for three volunteers to take charge of various aspects of the job. I volunteered to see that all luggage made it to the bus, and others took charge of gathering and guarding our specially issued Peace Corps passports. Late in the evening, I learned from Vivian that a latch on one of her suitcases had broken. I had packed, among other practical things, a six-foot length of rope which I used to secure her bag, a fix that held all the way to Bundu, the village where we would be living with families there, or in the neighboring village of Matshipe. Months later she was still using that rope to hold her bag together.

Our last night in Philadelphia a bunch of us, including the two Susans and Linda, went to a nice Italian restaurant and shared a bottle of good red wine in celebration of our amazing circumstances, thinking that it might be awhile before we again shared such a meal. I didn't sleep much after going to bed, and since we were all getting up at 1 a.m., nor did anyone else. I slept much of the ride to New York, making up a little for the short night before. Our flight didn't actually leave until about seven in the morning, so we had several hours to kill before boarding our long flight to Johannesburg. Some stretched out on the floor; others sat on suit cases and visited. I too spent some of that time getting to know some of my peers, including Doc Susan, who told me, but hadn't yet told the others that she was a physician. She asked me not to mention it to our new colleagues. Eventually, she shared it with everyone.

A couple of months into our placements, Doc Susan had to return home to care for her critically ill brother. He improved and she was about to return when a hurricane hit her Ohio town and her home and car were damaged by falling trees. She finally accepted that she wasn't meant to complete her service in Africa and stayed in the U.S. She'd had an unusual placement in the office of the premier of KwaZulu-Natal in the provincial capital city of Pietermaritzburg, only an hour south of my placement near the small city of Estcourt.

Linda and I spent a quiet hour or so before the flight playing cards, one of her favorite pastimes, and talking about our histories in the health field. She won every game.

4

Welcome to South Africa!

I don't remember much about the long trans-Atlantic trip, except that there were Peace Corps volunteers destined for Zambia sharing our flight. I do remember the arrival. John Jacoby, Peace Corps South Africa country director, who had been an airport administrator in New Jersey, and Bridget Hughes, training and development manager, who had been a fisheries volunteer in Zambia, greeted us outside the baggage claim area with handmade cardboard signs that read "Welcome SA 25" and "Welcome to South Africa." John had been a volunteer in Nepal in the '60s and had returned years later, with his adult children, to reconnect with people from his village. Bridget, like me, began thinking about Peace Corps service at a young age. Eventually, after getting a master's degree in social and cultural anthropology, at the age of thirty-five she became a volunteer. In Zambia she met Manda, who would become her husband. He owned a restaurant and three bars and educated his customers about HIV/AIDS, and passed out condoms.

A few minutes earlier I thought I might get left behind when there seemed to be a problem with my visa. While others were cleared through in seconds, the officer scrutinizing my passport didn't find what she was looking for. She kept telling me she couldn't let me stay in South Africa for more than ninety days without the proper visa. I explained that I was part of a group of American volunteers who would be in South Africa for more than two years, working in rural villages to help deal with the HIV/AIDS crisis. I pointed out numerous other volunteers who were being hustled through without issue. She called over a supervisor who questioned me further and examined my passport. After several minutes and after most of my colleagues had cleared customs and gone to look for baggage, they apparently found what they needed and let me through.

We gathered in front of the airport named for Oliver Tambo, a leader and contemporary of Nelson Mandela in the struggle for black independence. A large bus awaited us and we were greeted by Peace Corps South Africa training manager Victor Baker, who soon became one of everyone's favorite Peace Corps staff members. Victor had been with Peace Corps about five years. Before that he had been a teacher and a musician. He, like me, had been a single father who had raised a daughter. I never learned why Victor, a black South African, had such an American sounding name. But I did learn that he was a big admirer of Peace Corps, loved his job, and was passionate about teaching volunteers his country's history and culture, especially the struggle to end apartheid. His two-hour lecture about internalized oppression, several weeks into training, was one of the highlights for me.

Victor also was passionate about teaching us the South African national anthem, which, since 1997, has included Xhosa, Zulu, Sesotho, Afrikaans and English, the five most widely spoken of the country's eleven official languages. Many of us struggled with Afrikaans, a variation of the Dutch language that early white settlers brought to South Africa in the 1600s. Pronunciation can be difficult for non-native speakers. We practiced Nkosi Sikelel' Afrika (God

Bless Africa) almost daily in preparation for singing it at our swearing-in ceremony at the end of March 2012. We also had occasion to sing "The Star-Spangled Banner," and, surely, I wasn't the only one to drop a tear or two. The South African anthem, written in 1897 by Enoch Sontonga, a Methodist school teacher, had been a church hymn.

I'm sure many of us dozed on the two-hour ride to the camp where we were to complete nine weeks of training. After an hour or so we stopped at a roadside shop where people could buy snacks. Many of us had brought rand, the South African currency, procured by our local banks in the U.S., and had our first experience using African public toilets. Many toilets work poorly or not at all, are dirty, and except in nicer areas, are pit toilets. In the village where I eventually would live for a year, people called our outhouse "the loo," a nod to British influence in South Africa dating from the 1800s and early 1900s. I later told a couple of American friends who were thinking about coming for a visit, to "never, never, never" go anywhere without your own personal roll of toilet tissue, since most public stalls don't have any or, if they start each morning with it, it's gone by ten a.m. The exception was service stations next to major highways, which tended to be nice, clean, well-stocked, and usually had a cleaning person posted near the entrance to collect tips. I always tipped, since I suspect that was the main source of income for such cleaners.

Months later, on what must have been a slow day at Masiphile (my organization), when I was using the loo—nicer than most—it occurred to me that when men are using the toilet they are usually standing and the seat is up, which enables us to see the thumb-sized cockroaches, huge spiders and ants that routinely inhabit the underside of the seat. A view that women don't get to enjoy because they're sitting down—half-an-inch or less away from the critters beneath. Critters that sometimes explore.

I once got locked in the loo for ten minutes when the inside handle broke off and the door was locked. No one could hear me yelling so I had to climb through the window. I was lucky. Most outhouses don't have windows. We had a pretty decent concrete toilet at the Zungu compound where I would eventually live. Sometimes neighbors would stop in to use it. One day a man knocked on my door and asked if I had some newsprint. I offered him my roll of tissue, thinking he would be grateful and impressed. He wasn't. He preferred the newspaper. I guess, like me, he was a reader.

5

The Irrepressible Niki

Camp Bundu, in Mpumalanga (em-poom-a-LONG-ga) Province, was owned by the local governmental entity. Peace Corps had rented it for a few weeks, provided the owners fixed a few things and got caught up on the routine maintenance. It had a dozen or so rondavels where we would stay, two or three to a structure, for about five days until we would move in with our host families. Showers were in community latrines with cold water under minimal pressure. But for the most part, no one cared. It was like the summer or church camp many of us had attended as kids back in the states. Though it wasn't as nice as Camp Wi-ne-ma on the Oregon Coast where I went as a kid. Wi-Ne-Ma didn't have cobras. But, we were Peace Corps volunteers! We didn't do much more than sleep in the rondavels since our days were packed from early morning to late in the day with language and other training and various tasks connected with being Americans new to Africa. Mosquito bites by the malaria-carrying insects were a concern so we were given repellant coils to light in our sleeping quarters at night, but neither Donovan nor I could get ours to stay lit. Thankfully, there weren't many mosquitoes.

Meals were offered buffet style in the cafeteria, prepared by local women hired to cook for us. The food was *mnandi* ("delicious" in Zulu) and plentiful.

About the second or third day the medical people from headquarters, or "post," gave us necessary shots for tetanus, hepatitis, and rabies. There was no shot for malaria, though there are medications one can take prophylactically to make catching it more tolerable. Since I was going to an area in the foothills of a mountain range, not malaria country, I escaped having to take one of the two malaria medications. Those who did have to take one of them reported interesting and colorful dreams. Occasionally one reads about someone becoming psychotic after taking Mefloquine.

The medical unit visit was our first exposure to Arlene, a fiftyish certified nurse practitioner, who had been a Peace Corps medical officer in several other African countries before coming to South Africa. She had kids and grandkids in the Kansas City area and was married to Solomon, a native of Ethiopia and a Pretoria architect. Arlene was universally loved for her dedication to the volunteers' healthy experiences, her sense of humor, flexibility, and willingness to go the extra mile on behalf of volunteers, and her willingness to take Peace Corps volunteer issues to administration. I had the privilege of getting to know her better than most volunteers because she was the Peace Corps South Africa staff liaison to the Volunteer Support Network. This meant periodic meetings of all of us, some of them at Solomon and Arlene's home. Once we all went out to dinner at an Ethiopian restaurant and Solomon ordered so we could have a truly Ethiopian experience, including eating from community dishes with our hands, common in many African countries.

One shot that we didn't get after arrival in Bundu was for yellow fever. The South African government required proof of this inoculation before arrival in the country, so we all had that done in our home towns, at Peace Corps expense, about $150. Results were forwarded to Washington, D.C. I went to a local clinic that specializes in serving international travelers. The doctor had been around for a long time and had a reputation for competence, so I wasn't worried. But his "bedside manner" could have been better. He was nice, but reminded me of some of the clients with Asperger's Syndrome I had known in my professional life. Asperger's is on the autism spectrum and people with the diagnosis often are quite intelligent, but not known for their social skills. As he prepared the injection he told me, bluntly without the hint of a grin, "I'm obligated to tell you that for every one million people who get this shot, twenty of them turn yellow, vomit blood and die." He wasn't laughing, but the odds were good so I told him to go ahead. I survived to laugh and write another day!

At Camp Bundu and later at the nearby SS Khosanna Game Preserve much of our time was spent learning a "target language," the primary language spoken in the area where one would be posted. Mine was Zulu, or "isi-Zulu," the formal name of the language. In the beginning we met as a group and learned greetings and phrases in several languages, since we didn't know where we were going.

Our main Peace Corps supervisors, known collectively as "associate Peace Corps directors," or APCDs, had been reading about our backgrounds, skills, and work histories and had read the essays we were required to write as part of the application process.

They met with each of us a couple of times to talk about individual desires, and goals for service, answer questions and to get to know us so they could, theoretically, match each volunteer with the best possible organization. Not everyone was happy with his or her placement, and some were openly critical of their APCD's decision about their destination. But I'm one who tends to give the benefit of the doubt, and have always believed that Peace Corps staff did the best they could with what they had to work with. It's also true that one of those APCDs, mine, was fired a few weeks before I departed for the U.S. I never had any issues with him, but others complained that he wasn't responsive, especially to female volunteers. If it's true he wasn't as responsive as he should have been, it was an exception to the rule. My experience was that Peace Corps South Africa staff members were dedicated, hard-working, knowledgeable, competent, caring and often willing to go the extra mile to make things work for volunteers and to ensure they were successful in their placements. We often got emails that were sent well after five o'clock.

One of the most memorable days we experienced happened midway through PST when we were called to the front of the room, one by one, to accept a packet of information about the organizations where we would be placed. Staff had posted a huge map of South Africa on the wall so we could find our villages or closest cities and compare where they were in relation to others'.

I learned that my nearest fellow Peace Corps volunteer would be Kristen, a recently-graduated mechanical engineer from Albuquerque, who would be only about twenty kilometers away. Not far were the small cities of Winterton and Bergville, where several others, Peggie, Rachel, Andrea and Christopher and Emily, were to be placed. Ultimately, all those placements, except Kristin's, failed for a variety of reasons, but the volunteers were transferred to other programs. Andrea ended up the farthest away, in a different province, Limpopo.

But before that little group got separated we gathered in Winterton one weekend a month for several months at Friday night potlucks—what locals called a "bring and share" ("covered dish" in the Southern U.S.). They were organized by a couple of local Protestant ministers, who wanted to support the volunteers in the area. This included not just Peace Corps volunteers, but also young women from England, John's country of origin, and Germany, Elke's home. There was also a seventyish woman from Australia, Anna Marie, who was allowed by her Australian organization to drive a car, unlike Peace Corps volunteers, who were prohibited from driving. She volunteered at the same place, Isibani Community Center, where Peggie and Andrea served and was able to borrow a company car at times and take others on weekend adventures. I got to do that a time or two, with Peggie, sleeping Friday in a spare bed or on the floor at the Isibani volunteer residence, after the potluck. I traveled further than anyone else, taking two or three taxis to get to Winterton from my village. Since taxis don't run after dark, going home Friday night was never an option for me. One Saturday morning we gathered at the Pig and Blanket—no doubt owned by whites but staffed by blacks – for coffee while '80s Billy Joel tunes played in the background, including his hit, "The Longest Time."

It was in Bergville, which had a substantial white population, that Christopher and Emily, a couple of scruffy-looking Peace Corps volunteers from America, was approached by a white couple one Saturday at a public book fair. The man and woman were seeking information about the event, but were unwilling to talk to the nearby well-dressed black people who were clearly in charge. Christopher and Emily, who told this story at one of our training events, had to redirect the white couple to the people in charge. It struck me as perhaps a case of reverse internalized oppression—white people afraid, or unwilling, to interact with blacks.

Another memorable event for all volunteers came, five

days after we arrived at Camp Bundu, when we met the families we would be staying with for the next eight weeks. Staff had lined up chairs in three rows in the cafeteria for trainees, and, directly across, chairs in four rows, facing us. Rachel was missing. She had taken ill and was at the medical unit in Pretoria for treatment. The chairs across from us were for our soon-to-be hosts. There were couples, single men, individual women, entire families. Women holding a baby in one arm and the hand of a child in the other, older people, young ones. It was quite a scene with all of us scanning the crowd, trying to guess which person or family was ours, wondering how we would communicate with them, what their homes would be like, whether we would like the food they served.

The day before, in preparation for the upcoming Peace Corps pairing of trainees with families, Victor had told us how nice, or not, our host families' village homes would be. "A nice house won't teach you anything. It's the families, the people inside, who will teach you about South Africa." Most, if not all, homes had running water indoors (though it didn't always work), and most lacked indoor plumbing. Some homes were very nice, some were not. I suspect mine was somewhere in the middle. Some, though not mine, came with appearances by venomous snakes before training was over.

Greg and Pat, the older married couple from Seattle, who lived less than a quarter mile from me, came in one morning not long after we had moved to our village homes with a cell phone picture of a five-foot long spitting cobra, draped over a stick, that Greg had killed the night before by pelting it with bricks. The family dog, a Chihuahua, had been barking wildly in the backyard and when Greg went to investigate he found the snake trying to get away and the dog grabbing it by the tail. The snake would spit venom at the small dog in self-defense. The dog would let go and retreat and the snake would again try to get away. This happened several times, before Greg finally took control and dispatched the cobra. The Chihuahua's eyes had to be washed thoroughly. A few days later we heard from Susan, the Virginian, that her host father had been pressed into service the night before when a fifteen-year-old village girl had been sprayed in the eyes by a cobra. The host was the only person on the block with a car (*imoto* in Zulu) and was asked to take her to the nearest hospital, many kilometers away, for an overnight stay to get the treatment that would keep her from being blinded. Thank goodness for a national health plan. Greg's family insisted on burning the dead cobra, rather than burying it. Greg called the dog a hero.

Someone, Barigile perhaps, stood between the two sets of people and read off names one by one: the name of the volunteer, followed by the name of the family. Barigile (bare-a-GEE-lay) was the home stay coordinator and the main go-to guy when there were issues about housing during training. He was also the guy who tried to make sure that all thirty-six families got their promised delivery of several boxes or bags of groceries every two weeks in exchange for hosting and feeding their volunteer. Families got no other compensation for hosting volunteers. Some, I supposed, may have done it for the groceries—after all, this was an area with an unemployment rate above fifty percent—but most did it to meet an American and learn more about American culture. Some may have been motivated by a desire to improve their English. The night before we'd all gathered in the gymnasium to help sort a huge truckload of foodstuffs into thirty-six equal piles, one for each family, to be taken with us when we departed Camp Bundu for our new temporary homes.

Barigile, a trouble shooter of the first order, handled issues as diverse as a family missing a bag of carrots or a trainee's complaint that her family was not giving her enough food to keep her from being hungry.

Mid-twenties Texan Niki was the first volunteer to meet her family. Her behavior set the tone for the rest of us and made what may have been an anxious moment for some rather fun instead. When her name was called she jumped up, ran forward in all her amazing, outgoing glory and practically jumped into the arms of her new host mother. Both began to laugh and soon everyone in the room was laughing and clapping. Following the irrepressible Niki, everyone else, even reserved me, did the same. It was moving and brought tears to the eye of many. When my name was called, followed by "The Bhuta Family," Maria, a rather large, older woman, came forward, holding the hand of a boy I would soon learn was five-year-old Siyabonga, her grandson, whom she and her husband were raising. Siyabonga means "we thank you" in Zulu and is not an unusual name, since Zulus commonly name their babies something that has a specific meaning in the Zulu language, besides being a name. (As in Silence, the name of the driver who took me to Pretoria to return home).

The website africanholocaust.net described the importance of naming Zulu babies this way: "Naming of the infant is seen as an important part of the birthing rite, as it is believed that names have a spiritual vibration which affects the person as an infant, into adult life and beyond. The infant's name is given as a reflection of its personality or life mission. When an infant's name reflects his/her life purpose, it serves as a powerful tool and reminder of his/her life's work as whenever their name is called, it is a steady reminder of their mission."

Maria and I embraced, a little awkwardly, but soon we were standing by the wall, watching as the rest of the group met their families. I had greeted her in Zulu—"Sawubona ma," or "Good day, mother," but had failed to understand her response. Before long we were all loading our luggage and our grocery allotments into one of the Peace Corps' thirteen-passenger vans we would come to view at times as second homes since we spent so much time in them. It was a five-minute drive to the nearby village of Bundu, or Matshipe, for some, to begin our two-month home stays where our new families would help us learn our "target language" and teach us all they could about rural South African culture, about the black South African experience. Bundu and Matshipe were about seven miles down a dirt road from the nearest paved highway.

We had been at the Camp Bundu training site less than two weeks when one day after lunch we were assembled and told there was a schedule change for the afternoon and that John, the country director, had come from Pretoria to talk to us about something important.

A couple of months later I wrote a blog post; I had been posting them at my website from the beginning: *I'm going to tell a little story about something that happened early in training more than two months ago. I didn't tell this story at the time because I didn't want my friends and loved ones back home to be overly-alarmed, and because I wanted to save it for a blog post on how important safety and security is to Peace Corps.*

I went on to explain that John Jacoby was accompanied by John Allen, the regional safety and security coordinator for Peace Corps South Africa and seven other African Peace Corps countries. That "something" was that two nights earlier, armed intruders invaded the camp at 11:30 p.m. There was a gun battle, and one of the guards we had come to know had been shot in the stomach. Another guard was pistol-whipped. Both were in the hospital, the gunshot victim in serious condition. The robbers got away with a gun and a cell phone, but nothing else. No Peace Corps staff was injured.

John, who started his duties as country director only two months before our arrival, in November 2011, said he wanted to be completely open and honest about what had happened, to answer all questions, and to assure us that all necessary steps would be taken to keep everyone safe. He said that John Allen and our own Peace Corps South Africa safety and security coordinator, Gert (pronounced "hairt"), had evaluated the situation with local police and concluded that it was an isolated incident. They answered all questions clearly and honestly. Security was increased. The guards recovered, though the one who was shot was in the hospital for several days. Rachel, one of the PCTs from Virginia, volunteered to hand-make a nice card for everyone to sign. This was the first time I understood how important safety and security of volunteers is to Peace Corps, but it wouldn't be the last.

Training continued with no further significant security incidents.

A few days later we left the youth camp and moved to a different nearby venue, the SS Khosanna Game Preserve, which also had rondavels and nice meeting areas. We were told the change had nothing to do with the shooting incident, but that the local government that owned the youth camp had failed to follow through on promises in regard to other issues. In any case, "SS," as we came to call it, was a nicer place and gave us many opportunities to see African wildlife on the mile-long, twice daily drives from the main dirt road, down a smaller dirt road, to the center of the preserve. We saw wildebeests, water buffalo, baboons, monkeys, zebras and deer-like animals, the size of elk, that I never positively identified, but could have been elands. Or something else. Cool antlers, though! About two or three feet long and curved upward. Someone suggested they were impalas—*"springboks"* in Zulu. Springboks is also the name of the South African rugby team, made famous in the movie "Invictus" with Matt Damon as the team captain and Morgan Freeman as Nelson Mandela. Their colors are green and yellow, same as the University of Oregon Ducks in my hometown of Eugene.

Those first days were a whirlwind of activity, as we got to know each other, were introduced to our "language and cross-cultural facilitators," or LCFs, started to learn words and phrases of several of South Africa's many languages, and had our first tastes of Peace Corps life. That activity continued for the rest of the nine weeks of training. After five nights we went to live with our host families and came to the camp only during the day, by local taxis. There were armed security guards about, hired by Peace Corps to keep everyone safe and to look after the property, vehicles and other expensive equipment, especially at night. The shooting incident reinforced the importance of security.

In the ensuing weeks there were many more sessions that touched on safety and security in numerous ways: using public transportation like taxis, watching out for fellow volunteers when they might use poor judgment in public; in policies around alcohol use, not hitchhiking, and avoiding big cities, especially "Joburg," which was said to have a high crime rate. In fact, it's Peace Corps South Africa policy that volunteers not be in Johannesburg, ever, unless on official Peace Corps business or while in transit to Pretoria. I never had any problems traveling through Joburg, though I did see large rats rushing about in broad daylight.

Safety and security training also covered not going out at night and about being in pairs when possible, rather than walking alone. About always knowing what's going on around you, being observant. About not carrying large amounts of money and not flashing it, or your fancy laptop or camera, around. About letting others know where you are when you travel. Common sense mostly. But, as we all know, sometimes common sense isn't very common so Peace Corps staff hammered away at ingraining those ideas into our heads. Most of these sessions were led by Gert, a talkative, outgoing white guy who used to be a cop. And wore the most outrageous shirts! And rode a big motorcycle. And collected snakes. Still, by the time I left fourteen months later, several of my friends had been victimized in various ways, mostly theft, though there were also incidents of assault and severe sexual harassment. Linda's laptop was stolen from the cargo area on the plane on the flight from JFK to Johannesburg, presumably by an airline employee who may or may not have been South African. Fortunately, she had insurance that paid for its replacement.

Our last session on safety and security, a couple of days before training ended, covered the "emergency action plan" every volunteer is supposed to learn: what to do in a true emergency like major civil unrest, a coup, or a natural disaster such as a tornado or earthquake. There had been a coup recently in another nearby African country, Mali, and "due to ongoing political instability following a military coup" volunteers were evacuated. The State Department described the situation as "fluid and unpredictable." The Peace Corps has on several occasions over the years pulled out of countries, removing all volunteers more or less immediately, because of significant major, potentially dangerous events. Because volunteer safety is paramount. (In 1968 several Peace Corps Panama volunteers were detained and held incommunicado for several days, accused of spying and interrogated and jailed before eventually being released. Relations between the U.S. and Panama were strained for a time, and Peace Corps pulled out for several years). There are four alert levels, the most serious of which is to evacuate immediately to your predetermined gathering point, where Peace Corps staff will meet you and guide you to safety. It was at this session that John asked those of us who blog about our experiences not to mention the specific villages we were in, as a safety and security precaution, since Facebook posts and blogs are public forums, available to anyone with access to a computer. He didn't offer any examples, as I recall, about why it might be dangerous to announce where you're staying, but it was a request I honored. We were free to tell friends and family where we lived.

(On the day I wrote the last chapter of this book, February 24, 2014, Peace Corps announced that 200 education and youth development volunteers had been safely evacuated from Ukraine, a portion of which, Crimea, had been "invaded" by neighboring Russia, an action condemned by countries all over the world. There was fear that civil war between Ukrainians in support of Russia and those favoring an independent Ukraine would result. A few days later fellow SA25er Peggie, nearing seventy, announced she was leaving shortly for Ukraine to teach English for six months, and then would be going to Cambodia for a year to volunteer at an orphanage that included HIV-positive babies).

6

Propositioning Five Gorgeous Women for Unprotected Sex

Ever been to one of those workshops or conferences where they make you get in groups of five or six and act out a scenario, or have a small group discussion to make some important point or to teach you something? The theory is that if you act it out or talk about it in a small group, you're more likely to remember it. I've never liked those either. I've always preferred to listen to the speaker, take notes, and refer to them later as needed. If you're like that, you may not like Peace Corps training.

We soon came to see that Peace Corps trainers are firm believers in the practice of role playing, and small group exercises. I couldn't tell you the number of times we counted off by fives, or sixes or sevens so we could gather in small groups. Many of the younger trainees found this annoying and complained that they were being treated like young children, but we older trainees just smiled and saw that counting off was quick, simple and efficient. We would form groups, grab a piece of butcher paper and a marker and go off to a corner to do the exercise or role play. Someone would be the recorder and, when finished, someone else, sometimes me, would volunteer to represent our small gathering to the larger group where we would share the results of our work. This enabled us all to practice what Peace Corps trainers had been preaching to us, and for all to gain the wisdom of the several other groups.

I decided to embrace the training techniques and was an active participant in the process, sometimes recording on butcher paper, despite having handwriting that was not as nice as most. I made several presentations in nine weeks of training. Speaking of writing with markers, I was surprised to learn early on that of our original group of thirty-six, only two us were left-handed—me and Julie, from Rochester, New York, one of the youngest. This surprised me, since statistically somewhere around fifteen percent of the population is left-handed, and, in my experience, the percentage is even higher in groups of social worker types, which describes many of the people who join Peace Corps. When I worked at Lane County Developmental Disabilities Services I was once in a meeting where all were taking notes and eighty percent of us were lefties.

I think most of my fellow volunteers would describe me as a frequent contributor to the discussions. This would surprise my friends and colleagues back home who see me as pretty quiet in groups, especially in large group discussions (a woman once broke up with me because she said I wasn't social enough). We learned many mantras in training, like "learn and embrace patience and flexibility." My personal favorite, which probably didn't apply to anyone else, is the result of one of those role plays.

Early on, Arlene, the medical officer, was presenting health information about the importance of practicing what we would be preaching in our HIV/AIDS prevention work in rural villages: use condoms, whether you're having sex with a "host country national" or another Peace Corps volunteer. She said that exit surveys showed that forty percent of volunteers were sexually active within a couple of months of arrival in their countries, and that by the twentieth month the rate was close to ninety-five percent. I figured I would be one of the five percent remaining.

Since there were six men in the group, and thirty women, she instructed us to divide into six groups, each with one man. In my group were five women, all in their twenties, and me. My role—and the role of the other men—was to try to convince each of those women to have unprotected sex. The job of the women was to resist those efforts. Arlene called it the "condom game." Afterward, each group presented its findings. My new mantra/philosophy, when facing a new challenge in my Peace Corps experience, became, "If I can ask five gorgeous women in their twenties to have unprotected sex with me, I can do anything!" Some of those women had pretty creative ideas about repelling a man who insisted on sex without a condom, but I'll spare the details, including those offered by Jess, one of our SA25 leaders and openly lesbian. She became one of our early "ETs" when she returned to the U.S. to rejoin a new partner. But she had one of the more convincing arguments for not having unprotected sex. After that fun activity Arlene showed us a sobering video of five former Peace Corps volunteers from various countries that had become HIV-positive while in service, discussing their experiences and consequences of not using a condom.

A lot of our training was provided by staff from the U.S. Centers for Disease Control and Prevention, a Peace Corps partner, with several programs in Africa. They shared the latest cutting-edge knowledge and training on HIV/AIDS and delivered presentations that were fascinating. One day an African woman in her thirties, Thembeka, was talking about counseling and prevention, standard training for anyone working on the continent to prevent HIV. She asked for a volunteer to demonstrate the proper way, using a plastic model of a penis, to put on a condom. Jess stepped up to the plate, all the while joking about whether or not she would be able to carry out the exercise. We were all laughing, knowing her sexual orientation, a secret that Thembeka presumably didn't know. Jess did well for someone, presumably, so unfamiliar with penises and condoms.

Other training topics included the distribution of the Peace Corps medical kits, one of the more well-stocked first aid kits I've seen (everybody got one) and information on malaria and how to avoid it. We learned of the Peace Corp approach to development in countries like South Africa, the history of the country, economic disparity, appropriate behavior with host families, Participatory Analysis for Community Action (PACA), the heart of Peace Corps philosophy when working in developing communities, about HIV/AIDS, taught mostly by staff from the CDC; the history of race relations in both South Africa and the U.S.—how they are similar and how they are different— organizational behavior and local networking, group facilitation, strategic planning with non-governmental organizations (NGOs), stakeholder analysis; and professional behavior in the workplace.

One of the most interesting topics was internalized oppression—"When people are targeted, discriminated against, or oppressed over a period of time they often internalize (believe and make part of their self-image their internal view of themselves) the myths and misinformation that society communicates to them about their group. Often people experience this phenomenon unconsciously," according to The Community Tool Box, a program of the University of Kansas.

It's the opposite of empowerment, which is "the process

of increasing the capacity of individuals or groups to make choices and to transform those choices into desired actions and outcomes. Empowered people have freedom of choice and action. This in turn enables them to better influence the course of their lives and the decisions which affect them" (a definition used by the World Bank). There are parallels between U.S. and South African history in how both treated blacks in the past. The U.S. had slavery and South Africa had apartheid. Slavery ended in 1865 with the end of the Civil War, but, in many ways, an apartheid-like existence continued for many blacks, especially in the South, for another hundred years. Some would say it exists still. Such a culture of oppression is not easily overcome and might take many generations for there to be noticeable change.

The session on internal oppression was taught by Victor, the training manager, whom I described at the time in a blog post as "an amazing man." In one of our discussions about internalized oppression one Peace Corps staff member suggested that in some ways South Africa was still a "conflict zone," though there was not open warfare between various factions, as in the Democratic Republic of the Congo. But because it has been only a few years since apartheid ended, and there is still much anger and disagreement on both sides, that contributes to a sense of conflict. She offered it as a possible reason why SA25's dropout or early termination rate was higher than other Peace Corps countries. The average is ten to fifteen percent but ours, by the time I left, was thirty-three percent. Some people, like me, leave for reasons beyond their control, but most that "ET" choose to leave. Occasionally, a Peace Corps volunteer is "administratively separated" for inappropriate behavior or breaking significant rules, sometimes repeatedly. I can think of a few volunteers, perhaps one in my group, and some in others, who were "admin-sepped." I think the culture of sexual assault and sexual harassment that is prevalent in South Africa also contributed to our group's high rate. Most of SA25 were women and I would guess that every woman in the group was subject to blatant sexual harassment within in a couple of weeks of arrival in her village. Some had unwelcome marriage proposals.

In some circles in the Peace Corps world, a posting to South Africa is known as being sent to "Posh Corps South Africa." There may have been some truth to this when we were in Pretoria for training or meetings, and had the opportunity to go to a movie in a real theater or eat in a nice restaurant. But life in the villages certainly wasn't posh. I was reminded of the nickname for the Portland Campus of Oregon State Hospital, one of the state's several psychiatric hospitals where I worked in the public mental health system. Some called it "POSH," though it was anything but.

The session on economic disparity in South Africa was also memorable. Morgan, an APCD from the education program who lectured that day, was an enthusiastic speaker who was passionate about the subject. At the time I thought he was a visiting professor from one of the universities—I must have dozed off during the introduction. It would be a couple of weeks before I ran into him at post and learned that he was an APCD. On my last day in South Africa I encountered him at post and thanked him for the impression he left on me. Morgan's lecture followed Victor's on internalized oppression and he offered what I thought was a dramatic and telling example of the concept. He told the story of a volunteer in an earlier training group whose host mother would serve the white volunteer dinner, but then retreat to the kitchen to eat her own meal. She didn't consider herself worthy of eating in the same room as a white person.

The volunteer had to insist, repeatedly, that she join him at the dinner table.

Studying our target languages and learning about culture was a significant part of training. Led daily in small groups by LCFs, we learned about the culture from skits they performed, and from the discussions that followed our endless questions. They were true ambassadors of all aspects of the black South African experience. My LCF was Nonjabulo—meaning "happiness" or "excitement" in Zulu, but who went by the nickname of "Minky" since there was another LCF with the same name. She was close to a college degree in education and wanted to teach high school. She once asked me to review one of her papers about behavior issues in children when she learned I had a long career in mental health work. It was well-written and on target and needed minimal input from me.

I struggled to learn the Zulu language. The language sessions were the only part of training I didn't care for, though it was clear how important it was to being a successful volunteer and to becoming integrated in your new community. Jason Carter, President Carter's grandson, explained in his book, *Power Lines*, how he was only able to integrate into his black community as easily as he did because of how well he had learned the local languages—two of them in his case. He also said he seemed to have a natural knack, which I lacked, for learning language.

Moritz Thomsen, an older volunteer in Ecuador in the 1960s, in his book, *Living Poor*, described his language struggles in a way to which I could relate: "…after I had polished up the fundamentals of survival, a basic frustration of communication still remained. I could only go so far with smiles, titters, slaps on the back, little grunts of amazement and pleasure, happy foot stampings and soft-shoe shuffles.

This was fine for those superficial relationships that formed on a bus or in a store, but for the long haul—for the friendships that began to grow in my own village, in the house where I ate my meals, with the kids who swam with me almost every day—this inability to talk easily and deeply about ideas, convictions, prejudices was an infuriating thing. For we were, of course, very curious about one another, and we wished to probe each other to our own limits."

It was rumored that older volunteers had a more difficult time learning new languages than younger people did. That seemed to be my experience. My group included Christopher and Emily, the younger married couple from Seattle; Cara, a nurse, also from Seattle; and Sara, who was from Texas, but left early for Portland, Oregon because she didn't feel safe in her village and thought she could have a bigger impact in the U.S. She was also disillusioned by her organization's philosophy about using Peace Corps volunteers. "I would do the work, but not transfer any skills or teach people how I was doing things," she said in her email to SA25ers when she left. "That bothered me…They were not interested in me teaching them anything about how I did these things…I enjoyed the culture of Peace Corp but not of South Africa." Sara told us she liked science, especially research, and hoped to pursue it. A few months after I returned she posted on Facebook that she had been accepted into a PhD program in New Zealand.

Artistic Sara, and Alyssa, one of the other Oregonians in SA25, designed our group's tee shirt art, an upside down map of the world—with South Africa highlighted—and the phrase "Change The Way You See The World." On the back: Alyssa's contribution, the well-known AIDS ribbon, made in the colors of the U.S. and South African flags. (South Africa's flag is the only one in the world with six colors—red, white, blue, green, yellow and black).

Cara left for reasons similar to Sara's. In an email she sent to those of us still part of SA25 she said her reasons for leaving were, "…more about who I am and where I am gifted. I am a nurse to the core and I recognized that I need to be somewhere I can use those gifts and skills. I, unfortunately, did not have a good experience in the village and was removed after four weeks for long-term safety concerns. The incessant harassment and the acceptance of rape in my village also really got in my head." She said she hoped to return to Africa one day, perhaps to a different country, to work in nursing. It was not the first time and wouldn't be the last we would hear about or discuss the "culture of sexual assault" or the "culture of rape" prevalent in South Africa. Nor was it the first time a female 25er had to move to a different village because of sexual harassment—or worse. And it isn't just women who experience harassment. Matt, a veteran volunteer who was one of our trainers, told of giving his phone number to a local woman who then called him more than thirty times over two weeks.

All the others in my group seemed to do well at learning language. I often thought of a young woman I used to know who was fluent in Spanish by the time she graduated from high school in Eugene, then went on to major in linguistics—just like Chris from Seattle—and became fluent in French, German and Hebrew. She also invented her own language, "Irulian," when she was nine. She had the gene for mastering languages. I envied all their abilities. One evening after a particularly difficult day in language group, I wrote in my journal: *"I find myself with a knot in my stomach each morning, headed for language class, and feel like a fucking idiot*

*next to my peers, who are doing so well. I'm used to accomplish-
ing what I set out to do and it's enormously frustrating to do
so poorly at learning the language that is so important to my
success as a volunteer."*

We met almost every day for two hours at the home
of the family Minky lived with, across the dirt road from
my family, to study—vocabulary, plurals, "possessive con-
structs," locatives, noun classes, interrogatives, tongue
clicks. I absolutely understood the importance of learning
the Zulu language. But I struggled, despite what Nelson
Mandela said: "If you talk to a man in a language he un-
derstands, that goes to his head. If you talk to him in his
language, that goes to his heart"—the heart of Peace Corps
philosophy when it comes to learning local languages and
becoming part of a community.

I've always wondered if the training staff that made the
home stay assignments placed me with a family where no
English was spoken because they hoped that complete im-
mersion would help me learn faster. It didn't work, but, fortunately, except for staying with the Bhuta family during
training, most people I encountered in the villages spoke
passable English, so I was able to communicate with everyone but the very young and the very old; though I didn't
know this at first. And there were times when I misunderstood someone's English, or they misunderstood my Zulu,
and humor resulted. Minky was sympathetic and offered to
start meeting with me each morning a half-hour before everyone else arrived for some one-to-one, which helped. It
didn't help that we watched hardly any television at Bhuta's
house, though we had one. Other volunteers benefited in
their language learning by watching South African television, including "Generations," a popular South African soap
opera, a nightly event. We watched soccer matches occa-

sionally at my house, or news, though I never understood it. I did notice that each night on the evening news the broadcast always covered the three national sports—soccer, rugby and cricket. In the U.S. one rarely sees baseball, football, hockey or basketball covered at all on the national broadcasts, let alone all three each day.

7

The End of Training Approacheth

Toward the end of training, after we had learned where we were going, we had the opportunity to visit our new villages and meet our new supervisors at "supervisor training" in Newcastle, a good-sized city five hours' drive south of Mpumalanga. This event applied to those of us, which was most, being placed in KwaZulu-Natal Province. After that overnight training at a nice hotel-conference center, we would depart with our supervisors to spend four days in our new villages, the "site visit," meeting our new counterparts at the organizations, and have our first taste of village life outside our PST host families. Then we would return to PST for two weeks before actually moving to our villages. It was exciting, but also provoked anxiety. My Zulu was poor at best and I assumed I would have to communicate with many Zulus, though I didn't speak the language well.

Several hours into the ride to Newcastle in the Peace Corps kombi—the common name for a taxi in many African countries—the driver's cell phone rang. After a brief conversation, the driver handed the phone to me and said, "Victor wants to talk to you." I couldn't fathom why Victor would want to talk to me and I feared it was bad news about my elderly mother, not in the best of health, back home. But mom was fine. He asked if I would speak to the supervisors about the American work culture, which differs significantly from rural South African work culture.

We had learned from presentations and discussions with the LCFs that South African work culture wasn't what we were used to back home. We learned about "African time" and the phrase "This is Africa," often shorted to "TIA," to explain what happened when things didn't go as planned, which was often. TIA was often preceded by the words, "Oh, well." Relationships are important in black South African culture and it was not unusual for meetings to start late, for morning tea breaks to stretch to thirty minutes or longer, or for meetings or events to be rescheduled or cancelled because not enough people showed up. Counterparts at our organizations had to get caught up on village and family gossip, and fifteen minutes often wasn't enough time. Supervisors were just as likely as others to be guilty of this.

When it was my time to speak, I told how American workers are expected to show up for work on time, usually at eight a.m., work until five p.m., and accomplish much. I told them about fifteen-minute coffee breaks, morning and afternoon, that were expected to end after fifteen minutes. I told them meetings were expected to start at scheduled times, which caused murmurs from the audience. I said that Peace Corps volunteers were dedicated, hardworking people who probably expected to accomplish a lot in their new village assignments and would do their best to adjust to South African work culture, but also might at times behave as if they were back in the states.

The highlight of the first day was meeting our new supervisors. Nonhlanhla Radebe, the director of Masiphile Community Care Center, where I would volunteer for the next year, is a wonderful woman. (Masiphile means "healthy living" in Zulu). She is an attractive woman of forty-five who fits the description of many non-profit managers in the

U.S.: caring, thoughtful, supportive, intelligent, and willing to take on another task because it is the right thing to do. Never mind that her plate is already so full her "pap" is about to topple over onto the floor. The downside was that she isn't the most organized person and was always behind on deadlines or promises. She lost or broke at least three cell phones while I was there. More than once I was called upon to bail her out of an unexpected situation, including the time I had five minutes' notice before having to speak in front of 150 people, mostly children, about the importance of reporting child abuse to a responsible adult. Nonhlanhla had been held up in a meeting—one that no doubted started an hour late! I started speaking that day in Zulu, then had help from a translator. It went well.

We were given a few minutes to write down questions, then each couple—the volunteer and his or her new supervisor—were instructed to find a quiet place to interview each other. I tried repeatedly to correctly pronounce Nonhlanhla's name, but couldn't do it. Eventually I did, but it took a month to master. The "hl" sound in Zulu sometimes is pronounced as "sh" in English, but other times it calls for making a sound that can only be achieved by clicking the end of the tongue just so on the roof of the mouth behind the upper front teeth. I can do it perfectly to this day, but it took a lot of practice.

It was at this first meeting with Nonhlanhla that I learned of the many Masiphile projects. They included the home-based care program; the créche, or preschool, for children aged one to four; the community garden—part of its "food security" program; HIV-positive support groups for people; a parent support group; and elders' group. She told me that government funds for small monthly volunteer stipends had run out more than a year before, but that the volunteers had continued to work without the allotments. Her dream was for Masiphile to start the area's first-ever program to support orphans and vulnerable children.

It might have been at that meeting that she mispronounced "corps," as in "Peace Corpse". I corrected people, gently, a few times over the first few months, but finally gave up. I guess they just didn't understand the concept of silent letters common in words of French origin. Other volunteers told me it was common in their villages, too.

That night several us gathered in the hotel bar to review the day's events and wonder what tomorrow's trip to our new villages would be like. There was also talk about how Zulu men flirt a lot, especially with white women, and get away with what in the U.S. would be considered serious sexual harassment. From talking to veteran volunteers we learned that some single women chose to wear what looked like wedding rings because it was a way to ward off unwanted propositions. They could hold up their ring finger, point, and say, "I'm married!" Of course, that didn't stop some men, just as it doesn't stop some American men. We had learned that South Africa has one of the highest sexual assault rates in the world and the danger of sexual harassment or assault was very real and was discussed many times in training. Dan, the young reporter from Chicago, wanted to do his part to stem the harassment, so after he and the rest of us had consumed several beers, he suddenly got down on one knee in front of Cara and, in a loud, but sincere voice, proposed marriage and gave her a ring. We all cheered and clapped when she accepted. I think the rest of the people in the bar, mostly white, many of them probably Afrikaners, thought it was the real deal! They too clapped and cheered. It wasn't real of course; Dan was merely helping Cara avoid unwanted marriage proposals by giving her an out. It was a funny gesture. I wished I'd thought of it.

The next day we were ready to head out to the villages. Doc Susan was met by a high level administrator from the provincial government offices in Pietermaritzburg who had a chauffeur and a car that likely cost more than my first house. Susan was to work in his office, helping keep track of the provincial government's efforts to reduce the spread of HIV. It was a high profile position for a simple Peace Corps volunteer, but befitting a physician. Susan would have done an outstanding job if she'd been given the support she deserved. She spent most of the first several weeks going to hours-long boring meetings for "background," and never felt particularly supported by her organization. Although she eventually was placed in a nice apartment with indoor plumbing and reliable electricity, her earlier housing issues, in doctors' quarters on the grounds of a government psychiatric hospital, would fill a small book. The head psychiatrist told her unambiguously to demand different housing because her life would be in danger if she stayed there. I think Susan likely would have returned to Peace Corps from her family crisis in the U.S. if she'd felt supported at the premier's office.

Many volunteers left in cars driven by people from their organizations, but Nonhlanhla didn't have a car. She had arrived by taxi and she and I left by taxi, taking one from Newcastle to Ladysmith, another to Estcourt, my "shopping town" (about twenty-five kilometers from the collection of villages known as Imbabazane Municipality) and, finally, the local taxi to the village. It was nearly dark when we arrived at the family compound where her friend Sipho had agreed to host me for four days and where I would live when I returned in two weeks. It was a five-minute walk to Masiphile and I was to walk there the next day. We'd passed the center on the way, so I knew how to get there. That trip might have been the first time I heard of Ladysmith and its connection to Ladysmith Black Mambazo, a black, all-male choral group, formed in 1960, and made famous when they partnered with Paul Simon on his "Graceland" album in 1986.

The next day I was greeted by about fifteen Zulu women, dressed in colorful traditional garb, and one man: Mlamuli Hadebe, the volunteer gardener. What ensued was another highlight of my service: my new colleagues, virtually all of them volunteers, put on a traditional Zulu feast with chicken and pap, vegetables, and homemade Zulu beer, *umqombothi*, which is made from maize (corn), and sorghum. I was to enjoy it on many occasions in the coming months. They also danced traditional Zulu dances while I sat on a small, three-legged wooden stool – a kind that Zulu men traditionally use—while eating. Among the dancers was Noluthando ("with love," in Xhosa), who often went by Thando (TAWN-do). She was Nonhlanhla's daughter, thirtyish, petite, pretty, funny, married to Dlamini, an administrator at the municipality, and mother of three young children, who came to call me *"mkhulu"* or grandfather. Five-year-old Akhile, was her oldest and only son; her daughter, Asemahle, ("beautiful" in Zulu) was three; and Asevala, the baby, ("continuing" in Zulu), was born a few months before I came. Thando became pregnant again while I was at Masiphile, but miscarried after a few months. I also came to know Nonhlanhla's sister, Hlengiwe, who worked at the Nestle plant in Estcourt, and her two children. All treated me as family.

At this first meeting with the volunteers Nonhlanhla introduced me as Musa, which means "grace" in Zulu. It's customary in Zulu culture, when visitors come to stay in a village, to give them an appropriate Zulu name. (Musa was also the name given to Jason Carter, the president's grandson, by his village family). During my training home stay in Bundu I was called Oupa, the Afrikaner word for grandfather.

I also came to know Mlamuli well. He was fortyish and his wife had died a couple years earlier leaving him with three young children, who lived with relatives, but came to visit on school breaks. At times he started the cocktail hour early—common in rural South Africa where the unemployment rate is above fifty percent in many places. There the men have little better to do than gather in neighborhood taverns called "shebeens" and drink too much cheap beer. Shebeen comes from the Irish word "sibin," which means illegal whiskey, according to Wikipedia, and is used in many parts of the British Commonwealth. Initially, shebeens were illegal and were started as gathering places for blacks to meet and discuss social and political issues, since they weren't allowed in white bars. They represent a sense of community, identity and belonging, though historically they were closed down by police and the operators arrested. I had to walk by the shebeen in my neighborhood often and the men inside never failed to holler an invitation to join them. I never did, fearing their motivation was either to see if they could get the white guy drunk, or get him to buy a round of drinks—or both.

You could always tell when Mlamuli had been drinking as he would come into the building and be unusually talkative. Most of the time he stayed outside, quietly planting, watering, trimming or harvesting, or building things such as a netball court for the children who attended Masiphile's créche.

By the end of that first day I was exhausted, and full (*"ngisuthi"* in Zulu), but pleased with how the day went.

That night I stayed again in Sipho's family rondavel, this one much nicer, and bigger, than the one at Camp Bundu. Sipho's parents lived in Durban so he lived in the main house. The nice rondavel, where I was to stay, was made of gold-colored bricks and twice as high as most, with the traditional grass roof. A rondavel is round or oval in shape and traditionally made with materials that can be locally found. The walls are constructed of stones, stucco, cinderblocks or mud. The mortar may be sand, soil, or a combination, mixed with cow dung. The floor of a traditional rondavel is finished with a dung mixture to make it hard and smooth. The roofing elements are poles made from tree limbs, and the covering is thatch or grass, sewn to the poles with grass rope. It can take as little as one weekend or much longer to complete the thatch. A similarly-shaped structure, the yurt, is common in the U.S., especially out West. The first day back at PST after site visits I told the group that the rondavel I would be living in was "half the size of Yankee Stadium," which was of course a slight exaggeration. The floor was concrete.

8

Councilor Mkhize

That night at Sipho's rondavel, in the village of Mdwebu, I had a visit from one of the local ward councilors, a position similar to city council members all over the U.S., though locally elected officials in the U.S. aren't routinely assassinated as they are in South Africa. Mondli Mkhize (em-KEY-zay), a man about thirty-five, was a teacher at one of the high schools, and married to a social worker employed by the province. He described her as "very beautiful." They had two teen-age children. When he came to see me he was accompanied by two bodyguards, brothers, who were dressed better than other local men. Presumably, they were armed, though I saw no weapons. Mkhize, who like many Zulu men went by his surname, was a member of the African National Congress, the party of the late Nelson Mandela. He was also deputy mayor and it was this added level of responsibility that made him eligible for protection. I would also learn that in the previous five years, thirty-five local politicians in KwaZulu-Natal had been assassinated, many in drive-by shootings orchestrated by political rivals. Imagine thirty-five city council members in cities and towns in your state being murdered over five years. A couple of months before I left armed intruders broke into his home while he was alone and robbed him. He was uninjured.

Mkhize was a patron of sorts. Nonhlanhla had engaged his support in bringing Peace Corps to that part of Imbaba-zane, an area of 60,000 blacks in fifteen or so villages. I was the only white person (*umlungu*) ever to live there, accord-ing to Nonhlanhla. I came to admire and respect Mkhize a great deal and would have many interactions with him in the year I lived in his area. We often attended the same public events. The first time I spoke in front of an audience for Child Protection Week activities, I was able to introduce myself in Zulu and say that I was a Peace Corps volunteer from the United States—"Amelika"—and volunteered at Masiphile. Then I switched to English and Mkhize translat-ed the rest of my speech for me. There were eight police cars and at least twenty heavily armed and body-armored officers there. I didn't know if such a show of force was routine, or if trouble was expected. Despite the potential for danger or violence he was always responsive and willing to help sup-port any project, even though he was so busy with meetings and seeing to the needs of his constituents. That night in my rondavel, flanked by armed bodyguards, he thanked me for coming to his modest collection of villages and dirt roads to help his people.

He told me he had lived in KwaZulu-Natal his entire life and he spoke eloquently about the many problems the community faced: poverty, unemployment, teen pregnan-cy, drug and alcohol abuse, teens dropping out of school, HIV/AIDS. He said the solutions were "not just addressing the problems and fixing them, but getting young people to change their way of thinking." He pointed to his head and made a motion meant to represent a change in thinking. He got it, and I was impressed with his level of commitment in an area that had so many heart-breaking issues to deal with, and where it was so dangerous to be an elected leader.

Mkhize also told me that the serious traffic accident that Nonhlanhla and I had witnessed on our way from Estcourt the day before had resulted in two fatalities—the taxi driver and a woman Nonhlanhla later identified as one of her aunts. South Africa has the highest traffic fatality rate in the world and before my fourteen months were over, I would have several close calls involving vehicles that would lead me to believe I was lucky to have escaped death—multiple times.

My meeting with Mkhize ended with his promise to check in regularly. He gave me his cell phone number and told me to call him if there were problems I needed help with. As I watched him drive away I thought that people like him were the future of South Africa, that South Africa was lucky to have him. I would need his help sooner than I could have imagined.

9

Mdu and Amanda

The next three days were a whirlwind of activity as Nonhlanhla took me to the municipality, the library, the clinic and to meet the *induna*, sort of like an executive assistant to the *inkosi*, or chief. In our case, the inkosi was a woman because her husband had been the inkosi before he died and she took his place. Later Nonhlanhla would also take me to the nearest high school to meet the principal and to the Chicken Licken restaurant in town to meet with the Masiphile board president, Nora, a retired principal who had been one of Nonhlanhla's teachers when she was growing up in her village, Sobabili. Once the induna had given his approval, I would meet the inkosi.

But first, a trip to the municipality to meet as many local government officials as we could cram into an afternoon, starting with Beckie, an intelligent, attractive thirty-five-ish woman and an administrative assistant with a variety of responsibilities. Hers was also the first of several marriage proposals I would experience. She was one of several people I met who had chosen a Western name, though each also had a traditional Zulu name. I never learned hers, though we often rode the same taxi because she lived in Dutch, the village across the main "tar road" from Goodhome, my village. When Nonhlanhla introduced me Beckie smiled, shook my hand and said loudly, in perfect English, "I'm not married!"

I said, just as loudly, "Neither am I! What do you suppose that means?" She laughed and I asked, "Was that a marriage proposal?" She said it was and that later she would call me to "complete the application to be your wife." We talked many times, but the subject of marriage never came up again, so I guess she was joking. After that brief meeting with Beckie I was introduced to Michael Dladla, the manager of "youth, sports, gender and disaster planning." I was pretty sure there was no similar job title back in Eugene.

Later that day I met a woman about my age who was a member of the Masiphile support group for women who were HIV-positive. When we were introduced she promptly told me she had a twenty-four-year-old daughter who would make a good wife for me. At first I thought she was joking, just as Beckie had been, but she wasn't laughing or smiling. I told her what I would ultimately tell several women: "I'm honored that you would think of me in those terms, but I came to Africa to volunteer, not to look for romance." Later, when I discussed this with Nonhlanhla, she assured me the woman was serious in offering her daughter's hand in marriage, presuming I would offer the family the proper number of cows. This is a tradition called *lobolo*, in which a man honors a woman's family by presenting them with cattle, the most conspicuous sign of wealth in traditional Zulu culture. She said eleven cows was the appropriate number, which would be valued at about 40,000 rand, the currency of South Africa, or about $4,100 U.S. The woman likely was thinking of her family's long-term welfare and when she would no longer be able to care for them. Like most rural South Africans, the woman no doubt assumed that because I was white, male and American, I was rich. By her standards, I was. A few months later a young man who worked at the "tuck shop," or small store I patronized, offered me his twenty-nine-year-old sister when he heard I didn't have a wife or girlfriend. I told him that in America only the woman could make that decision; her brother couldn't do it for her. He laughed. "Besides," I said, "I probably couldn't keep up with her."

Later Nonhlanhla and I walked to the Ntabamhlophe Clinic and waited twenty minutes to see Mrs. KC Zondo, the woman in charge, who told us brusquely she didn't have time to talk to us. But, she relented when I said I would appreciate a few minutes of her time to tell her about my purpose. Mrs. Zondo, whom I would see again in a couple of days at my first church service, was a heavyset woman in her fifties who clearly was stressed by the enormity of her job. She led us to a cramped office where I told her about Peace Corps and asked what she needed most to help her clinic. She mentioned supplies, but said that what she needed more was additional staff like nurses.

"The problems and needs get worse each day," she told me. "We have 6,000 patient contacts a month (about 225 a day, Monday through Friday) and the numbers are increasing." She explained that they see many babies and young children every day, do pre-natal exams, HIV testing and counseling, and do the initial screening for medical male circumcision (MMC) procedures (though the surgery was done at the hospital in Estcourt), and see the same sort of cases that clinics, urgent care programs and emergency rooms all over the world see: accidents, sickness, bloody noses, broken bones and whatever else walks in the door or is brought in by ambulance. Encouraging men, especially young ones, to have a medical male circumcision is a relatively new addition to HIV-fighting tool box. We were told in training that studies by the Centers for Disease Control and Prevention show that an MMC reduces female to male transmission of the virus by up to sixty percent, essentially eliminating the flap of skin that would otherwise harbor and keep the virus alive.

At the library I met a young man of twenty-five, Nkosi-yomusa Phungula, who went by the nickname Mdu. He and his family also lived in Goodhome, a short walk from where I lived. I made the trip often as Mdu and his relatives became some of my best South African friends and I had dinner with them many times. They treated me like family and once invited me to an annual music event, the White Mountain Folk Festival, a few kilometers up the road. Often we would sit in the mud hut that was the family kitchen and visit while dinner was prepared by Mdu's wife, Amanda, or when the younger children were given their baths. I got to know Amanda (pronounced a-MON-da, which means "fit to love" in Zulu) well, as many was the time Mdu would invite me to dinner when I stopped by the library during the day, but then forget to call Amanda and tell her I was coming. He would be delayed working late or playing soccer with his friends, and I would arrive, to Amanda's surprise, and we would talk until Mdu got home. She was intelligent, caring, thoughtful, well-read and spoke English fluently, as did Mdu. She followed the news and saw the importance of education. Like many African parents, and parents everywhere, she wanted a good life for their daughter and for Mdu's nephews.

One night she told me about a job she'd had at one of the clothing stores in Estcourt. She liked her job, but hadn't been there long when the manager, a married man of about forty, told her bluntly that if she wanted to advance in the company, or keep her job at all, she would have to succumb to his sexual advances. She quit when she learned that the other female employees had had similar experiences. Some of them no doubt cooperated to keep jobs they needed to support their families. If there are rules or laws in South Africa about hostile work environments or sexual harassment, I never heard about them or saw them enforced.

Another night Amanda and I were sitting on the stoop waiting for Mdu when one of his friends stopped by. The young man was upset and sad because one of his friends had committed suicide the day before. He said he thought that many deaths reported as something else were actually suicides.

Mdu and Amanda had gone to school together in the village and had a six-year-old daughter, Eyami ("mine" in Zulu). I took her picture and posted it on Facebook on her first day of first grade. Like many young African couples, they referred to themselves as married, though, technically, they weren't because of the cost of the lobolo, which happens before marriage. There are also significant costs to a traditional wedding, which might include hundreds of people, the slaughter of a cow and several goats and chickens, special food, all the trimmings that would go with it, and many gallons of home-brewed Zulu beer. Amanda had no living family except two brothers who lived in distant cities, one of whom died unexpectedly at the age of thirty-one a few months before I left. Mdu's mother, Thandazile, who was about my age, lived with them, as well as Mdu's younger brother and two sisters and their children. Some couples settle for a simple civil ceremony at city hall, just like some couples in the U.S., but Mdu and Amanda had not opted to do that.

The first several times I went to dinner at Mdu and Amanda's, it was for Mdu to help me improve my Zulu-speaking skills, and for me to work with Nokulunga, one of his sisters, who wanted to improve her English. His other sister, Gugu ("precious" or "treasure"), and a brother, Lindokuhle were still in high school. I offered to pay Mdu as a tutor, an expense Peace Corps would have covered, but he refused. One night, when we were sitting in his bedroom and he went to another room to get something, I hid a twenty-rand note, about $1.80, in one of his shoes! Another night, as we were walking back to my place (Mdu insisted on escorting me if it was after dark) we talked about the proclivity of black South African males to cheat on their wives or partners. He said that when the couple didn't live together, ninety-nine percent of men cheated on their partners. He guessed the cheating rate by women was about sixty percent. I guess when you live together it's more difficult to hide unfaithfulness. Not being faithful to one's partner is, of course, a significant reason why the HIV/AIDS rate is as high as it is in South Africa. Faithfulness, along with practicing safe sex, was one of the messages we always delivered as Peace Corps volunteers.

It was on another of those late-night escorts home that I asked Mdu about the prominent scars on his cheeks. Many Zulu men, though not all, have such scars, in various configurations. Mdu explained they were part of ancient Zulu culture and made by his family with a razor blade when he was three weeks old. He said that when they heal if they are wider than when they were inflicted, that means the father of the boy isn't really the biological father, proof the woman cheated. If the scars are thin, however, this means the baby is the son of the stated husband. My reaction to all this, according to my journal?…"Amazing."

He also told me there is a parallel ritual for girls that involves cutting off the end of the baby girl's left pinkie finger with a sharp knife, on a wooden stool next to a "cow pie". If the end of the tiny finger falls into the cow pie, but can still be found, this means the child is the biological daughter of the named father/husband. But, if the digit cannot be found in the cow pie, or stays on the wooden stool, the real father is the woman's lover. *"Even more amazing,"* I wrote in my journal later that night. I had noticed that one of the women in Mdu's family had an abbreviated pinkie but didn't understand why until Mdu's lesson in culture.

If the ritual shows that a son or daughter does not belong to the woman's husband, Mdu explained, the child can be given to the family of the woman's lover. I didn't have the nerve to ask if this ritual is still practiced, or if it had played out in his family, but hoped it was a thing of the past. I did a fair amount of Internet searching to find more information about this odd cultural tradition, and to confirm I had the details right, but I found no references to such a ritual. What I did find were explanations that such cutting identified the bearer of the scars as being from a particular clan or tribe, indicating there is variation in how and why individual clans have such rituals.

Another time Mdu told me about being robbed by three armed men—one with a gun, another, a knife, and the third a club, while walking home from work after dark. He didn't recognize them but thought they might be brothers. They took his money, five rand (about 45 cents), and his phone, shoes and shirt. He was about to give them his pants, as ordered, when headlights illuminated them and the men ran away. He said he didn't report it to police because "there was no point," and that the police wouldn't or couldn't do anything about it. It wasn't the first time, or the last, I heard a low opinion of the South African Police Services.

Most of our conversations took place not on those walks in the dark, but in the Phungula family's mud hut kitchen. Such kitchens were common throughout Goodhome, and also typical of most rural South African villages. Villages where, even if electricity was available, most families cooked over wood-burning stoves. The cost of electricity was expensive for families where most adults were unemployed, or supported by the social security payment of one elderly person. Unlike in the U.S. where your local utility sends you a bill every month, for the power you used, in rural South Africa you have to pay in advance, get a code, and enter it into your meter to show the amount you paid before the power magically returns.

I know of one family where four generations live together and all are supported by the grandmother's monthly check. The twenty-eight-year-old mother of two young boys who lived there spent many hours each week seeking employment in an area where she might be competing with hundreds of equally talented and hard-working people for the same job. It's also common in Zulu culture for people in positions of authority to favor friends and relatives, which makes it even more difficult to get a job if you don't have such a relative.

The smoky, wood-burning stoves mean that village women spend many hours each week walking long distances to gather wood for cooking and for heat. And those stoves are incredibly unhealthy. More children under the age of five die of respiratory illness in Africa than of malaria, tuberculosis and AIDS combined. One potential project I identified in Imbabazane was to try to bring healthier, more efficient, wood stoves to my villages, perhaps those promoted by Stove Team International, a non-profit headquartered in my own city of Eugene. Stove Team has stove projects in Mexico and Central America that help people identify local materials that can be used to keep construction costs low. Their efforts have helped reduce mortality rates from respiratory illness and accidental burns related to cooking on open fires. I'd been in communication with Stove Team by email and they had expressed interest in expanding to South Africa. I had also joined the local Rotary club in Estcourt to see if they would be a local sponsor, but when my service was cut short I had to return abruptly to the U.S.

My four-day visit to Imbabazane ended with a Saturday trip to Giants Castle Provincial Park, that I would describe as almost as beautiful as Yosemite National Park, but without the 10,000 cars a day. I was also invited by Nora, of the Masiphile Board, to attend her church on Sunday. The park features dioramas of the earliest South African settlers—from thousands of years ago—the natives known as the San. Nora said she would meet me at the church at 7:30. She arrived at 9, but I'd introduced myself to several people, including the administrator of the local clinic I'd met earlier. She offered me a peanut butter and jelly sandwich, something volunteers made to serve when there was a break in the long service. Another church-goer, a woman about my age, offered to marry me when she learned I was single, explaining she knew I needed a wife to cook for me. She had a hard time believing me when I told her I had cooked for myself for many years. She may have been joking, but, like the woman from the HIV support group, she didn't laugh or smile.

The next day I was to take a ten-hour bus ride on Greyhound back to Bundu to complete my training before I returned to the village for my two-year commitment. I had a hard time understanding Nonhlanhla's directions about where to catch the bus in downtown Estcourt. I knew where the busiest intersection in town was from when I'd been there to meet Nora, but I was baffled by Nonhlanhla's explanation that the bus stop was "two robots up Harding Street" from the Chicken Licken. Two robots? "Do you mean two traffic lights up Harding Street?" I asked her. She smiled and laughed.

"Yes!" she exclaimed. The word "robot" and the long, twice-daily tea breaks (tea often sweetened with two to three heaping tablespoons of sugar) were both inherited from British influence…along with driving on the left side of the road. At our debriefing the next day I told my story of the several marriage proposals and Victor told me to "be careful," because, "you look like Sean Connery. You could find yourself married," he laughed. Someone else told me I look like "a cross between Sean Connery and Bob Hope." I laughed and reminded her that Bob Hope was dead.

My pre-placement visit to Imbabazane had been interesting, eventful, illuminating, and at times funny. But not everyone reported similar experiences.

Emily and Christopher had arrived at their organization to find that the administrator who had agreed to have them as volunteers wasn't there any longer and that no one was expecting them. The new person wasn't interested in having volunteers. Emily and Christopher were rescued by the NGO that was hosting Rachel. They said they were taken around their new town, Bergville, to meet the inkosi and others. The inkosi was a thirtyish man wearing a flowery shirt. He appeared to be drunk or high, hallucinating and swatting at nonexistent flies. He rambled and raved about once being in exile in another country in the '80s, implying it was for political reasons. At one point he became angry at his phone and threw it on the ground. They later learned that he had actually fled in support of a relative who was fleeing the law. Eventually another placement was found for Chris and Emily. They were pleased and thought their time in Bergville was productive. Rachel was forced to leave because of extreme sexual harassment and ended up living in a village not far from mine. We shared a post office box in Estcourt before she left for good. I packed up her possessions for shipment back home to Virginia.

Teresa was disappointed that she had been assigned to an organization primarily involved in home-based care—rather than a program that supported children, as she had hoped. But she was determined to make it work. Her new supervisor asked her for money twice. Susan from Virginia liked her placement, but Cara from Seattle learned that her placement would mean that a thirty-five-year-old woman would have to sleep on the floor or the couch. However, all her clothing, television and other possessions would remain in Cara's bedroom. Vivian from Texas, our senior member, was expected to stay in a dirty rondavel with broken windows. The next day, near the end of training, I more-or-less flunked my final language test, scoring in the lowest of eight possible levels. I got four of thirty-four questions correct. *"I'll bet mine was the worst score in the place,"* I wrote in my journal that night: *"Must study intently."* I couldn't wait to get to my village and find a tutor.

10

A Herd of Americans Under a Tree

Living in a Zulu village for a year after training was an amazing experience. The time we spent in training—befriending other volunteers from all over the U.S., living with host families, meeting hard-working, dedicated Peace Corps staff, being exposed to and absorbing the details of a dramatically different culture, traveling down dirt roads in cheap public transport to see wonders of the world—was in a class by itself. Younger people with their futures in front of them were having what might well be the most amazing experiences of their lives. Many of the older people like me, with most of our lives behind us, probably thought we would never again have such a dramatic life-changing experience.

And then there was Cindy from Ohio. The only one of us in our forties, Cindy was a hefty, healthy, outspoken woman, an animal lover, who defied stereotypes and stood out for reasons other than her age and her size. I can't speak for others, but when people started dropping out and returning home, as some always do, I doubt I was the only one who thought that she also wouldn't make it. The heat, the dirt, the gastrointestinal issues that are common when a Westerner moves to a developing country, the eye-opening cultural differences, the long travel in falling-apart taxis to get to meetings in Pretoria, the sexual harassment. Those things and others defeated many. But not Cindy, who also had a few marriage proposals. She flung aside stereotypes in multiple ways, not the least of which was what's known in the U.S. as being "conservative". She and I never discussed our political affiliations but if I were a bettin'man—and I am—I'd lay odds that she was probably the only one in our group who was registered to one of those conservative parties that say Peace Corps volunteers are liberal "bleeding hearts." I doubt anyone has ever called Cindy that. She always spoke her mind, probably in ways that were offensive to some. She was stationed in a remote, northwest corner of KwaZulu-Natal and had to ride in dusty taxis and buses more hours than most to get to Pretoria. My hat is off to her – but not for long, lest that African sun burn the top of my nearly naked head! She's one of a kind.

Cindy may have been with a group of about fifteen of us one Sunday afternoon near the end of training who decided to grab a taxi and head into the town of Kwaggafontein— often shortened to "Kwagga"—to do some shopping. It was hot and humid, as summers in Mpumalanga tend to be, and we were waiting for a taxi at the dusty roadside in the middle of the village. Someone suggested we move to the shade of a nearby tree in front of one of the local tuck shops, the small stores that sell basics like junk food, canned goods, cleaning products, bread, fresh fruit; cigarettes and, occasionally, beer. Someone worried the taxi driver might not see us. But Lilly from San Francisco, daughter of a doctor and a lawyer, was right when she said she doubted the driver would fail to see "a herd of Americans under a tree." She was right. He saw us and we made the twenty-kilometer trip to town without incident, though there was that giant stop sign the driver blew through at forty miles an hour. Peggie declared that a stop sign was a "suggestion" to a South African taxi driver. Many of us wanted to call home from the only phone booth for miles, reload on supplies, and/or find favorite fast foods—KFC and McDonald's being popular restaurants there. Some of us just needed a break from studying our target language or, in my case, from doing laundry, by hand in cold water, line-dried, a favorite Sunday afternoon activity. I needed a haircut and beard trim before swearing in so also that afternoon I hooked up with Senele, one of the LCFs, who had offered to introduce me to Antoin, a local barber. A shop was attached to his house next to the village cemetery where cows often grazed. He cut my hair and trimmed my beard for ten rand, about a dollar, while he and Senele visited. He did a great job and it was a helluva a deal. I wanted to give him fifteen rand, but Senele discouraged it, so I followed the oft-dispensed advice about not acting like a rich, over-generous American.

That might have been the "Kwagga" trip that was also the day of Lilly's mother's birthday. A bunch of us had gathered around the only phone booth in town. Lilly hadn't yet purchased phone service or a card that could be used with the public phone so I gave her my card to use. It was still early in the morning in the Western U.S. and her call had awakened her mother. They spoke for nine minutes, all the time that was left on the card. When she hung up she was crying, but happy. I called my daughter, Megan, the next time I was in town. The wait was worth it to watch and listen to Lilly's animated and joyful conversation with her mother.

That night, I wrote in my journal about a vivid dream I'd had about Doc Susan, the cardiologist, in which she *"kissed me passionately, in front of our group, surprising everyone, including me ...wonder what that means?"* We had recently sat side by side on a field trip to Pretoria and had a chance to learn more about one another. I liked her a lot.

She was about my age, maybe a couple of years older, and was unmarried and had a thirty-something daughter back home, just like I did. *"She's nice, attractive, intelligent, caring and has become a mother figure to a couple of the younger women,"* I wrote, adding, *"I can see how someone could fall for her."* I was quite disappointed when she ET'd a few months later.

Another favorite Sunday past time was to walk a mile or so to the river and sunbathe or wade, often with bottles of cheap wine in tow. However, one of us would eventually be diagnosed with schistosomiasis, a disease common in developing countries that is caught when microscopic parasites in rivers and lakes worm their way into the skin and into body organs. Few people die from it, but it's a chronic illness that affects many in places like rural Africa. The treatment is a course of an antibiotic that departing Peace Corps volunteers in South Africa are given whether they show evidence of the disease or not, since the symptoms are common in many illnesses and may not show up for a while. Because I left suddenly I had to have my treatment when I returned to Oregon. However, it took a week for the local pharmacy in my daughter's small town to get the medication.

Those Sunday strolls to the river or other walks around Bundu sometimes involved hooking up with Gary, the female Basset Hound that lived with the family of Andrea, the nurse from New Jersey. Gary followed Andrea most mornings from her family's house to the main road where we caught the taxi to the training site. I never learned how a Basset Hound made its way to a remote African village, let alone how a female dog came to be named the very un-African name of Gary. But she seemed to be a family pet, unlike most African dogs, which are seen as cattle or goat herders, or are used for security, or are just hungry homeless strays, foraging through villages for the same food wild animals seek. The athletic, mountain-climbing Cara, who lived on my street in Bundu, was a runner, but had to change her early morning running routine when a vicious dog kept chasing her.

The family I lived with later in Goodhome had two dogs. They had a role in security, their barking supplementing the safety provided by the six-foot high fence, topped with two feet of razor wire, but were also treated as pets and were well fed by the family. The dogs were always nice to me—too nice at times, jumping up with their muddy paws. I told them to stay down, which they didn't. Then one day Spamondla, one of Mr. Zungu's nephews who lived at the compound, laughed and pointed out what should have been obvious to me: the dogs didn't understand English. If I'd been scolding them in Zulu my words may have been more effective. But the word for "no" in Zulu, *"cha,"* was a word that called for a tongue click I never mastered. I often avoided such words.

On one of the Sunday afternoon walks to the river we were throwing a Frisbee back and forth. When Donovan threw the Frisbee to me it fell several feet short. I dived for it, on the paved road, and did a summersault. I came up with the disc in hand, but at the expense of a patch of skin on one hand and a sprained ankle. A dive like that came to be known as "taking a Niki," in honor of Niki's frequent dives while playing lunchtime soccer games during training. If records for skinned knees had been kept, I'm sure she would have been the winner.

Training also included several field trips, some for pleasure to shopping malls in Pretoria. Others were to help us learn about South African culture, both white and black. The most memorable trip for me was our visit to the Apartheid Museum in Johannesburg. Built in the late nineties by a casino company as a way to show what it was like to live under apartheid, it illustrates Twentieth Century South African history. The displays and pictures were sobering reminders of the cruelty and death perpetrated upon blacks by the whites, over the several decades before democracy arrived in 1994.

We also visited the Voortrekker Monument, a huge granite structure, built on a hilltop near Pretoria to honor the Afrikaners who began to emigrate from the cape colonies in 1835. The Afrikaners moved north to settle what eventually would become South Africa, looking for better land to develop their farms and ranches. Many of them were also motivated to escape what they considered the onerous British influence. Voortrekker is the Afrikaner word for "fore-trekker," or "one who pulls ahead."

On one of our trips to the city several of us tried to get cash from ATMs with our Peace Corps-issued debit cards that had been loaded with our first stipends. But many of the cards wouldn't activate, and hadn't for weeks, though Peace Corps administration insisted they should work. Jeff Prickett, director of management and operations, had a well-earned reputation for being organized, responsive, thorough, flexible and attentive to the needs of volunteers. He had been a Peace Corps volunteer in the African country of Gabon, 1999 to 2001, and had been a Peace Corps staff member in Chad before coming to South Africa. He was the only Peace Corps volunteer in his small group to make it to the end. The rest, about seven, ET'd before finishing their two years of building schools in the jungle. I got to know him pretty well. We both were writers and I enjoyed his book, *Pursuing Peace*, about his Peace Corps experience. Eventually, he married Rose, an African woman from Cameroon, whom he met while a volunteer. He adopted her boys and they had children of their own. Not long after I left he ended his long Peace Corps career and became an academician at Stanford University, not that far from Eugene.

I wrote in my journal that night: *"My only goal for the day was to get my debit card activated."* Pat and Greg and I and several others went to the mall's First National Bank branch and politely spoke with a customer service representative, an African woman, who truly wanted to help us. There were about fifteen of us trying to get our cards to work. She called bank officials at offices in other locations and hounded them to do their jobs and activate those cards. After about ninety minutes, her persistence paid off and we all were able to get cash from the ATM. She had accomplished in ninety minutes what Peace Corps had been unable to accomplish in six weeks. I went to a candy store I had passed on the way to the bank, bought a bag of gourmet chocolates, returned to the bank and presented them to the woman. Greg paid for half. She was speechless. I thought she would cry. We left the bank and a couple of minutes later I got an anonymous text on my cell phone: "U made that woman's day. Thank u so much!!!" To this day I don't know who sent me that message, though I've always suspected it was Cara from my language group. I still have that text stored in my phone.

Another field trip involved driving for an hour to visit NGOs that were similar to the ones most of us would be assigned to. We toured facilities, visited with children in crèches, talked with staff. The most memorable one for me was an organization that provided home-based care to people with chronic illnesses like HIV/AIDS. We sat in a circle on folding chairs and listened to the program manager and others tell us about what they did. When they were finished, a board member described the board's role and told us that members never served more than two or three years because that was how long it took for them to figure out how to steal money from the NGO. At first I thought he was joking but, like the women who proposed marriage, he wasn't laughing or smiling. He was serious. The manager, a woman named Ayana, *"should run for public office,"* I wrote in my journal. *"She was a master at rambling on and answering any question but the one asked."* The word bombastic came to mind. Or "chocolate-covered bullshit," as one of my friends in Eugene used to say about political speeches.

Another of our field trips to Pretoria was to visit Peace Corps headquarters, post, to learn about the Information Resource Center, meet Peace Corps staff and hear from veteran volunteers who were nearing their end of service. The IRC was overseen by KZ – pronounced Kay-zed, because the letter "z" is given the British pronunciation "zed." He was also in charge of logistical matters involved with training. I often envisioned him as a juggler, managing about a dozen things at a time, never dropping any of them, to make our training and goal of having our village experience be successful.

One volunteer we met was Andrew, from an earlier group, who, I learned, also had his home stay with the Bhuta family in Bundu during training. "I still hate that little bastard," he told us, referring to five-year-old Siyabonga, when he learned I was staying at the same place. Siyabonga could be annoying at times, but much of that was normal behavior for a child his age. Some of his acting out, I believed, reflected anger at his mother, who came by to visit occasionally, but lived somewhere else in Bundu. He missed her and had "abandonment issues," as we say in mental health. Of course, there was that time he urinated on my shoe when I wasn't looking…but most of the time he was tolerable!

Later we went to one of the malls for dinner and shopping. Andrew walked by as we were ordering at a Greek restaurant. We invited him to join us and I bought him a beer. He had a lot of negative things to say about Peace Corps and Jasmine, who went by Jazzy, called him on his obnoxious behavior. He said he was "just being honest." Upon further prodding he acknowledged that he'd had some good experiences, but that he "didn't like the African culture," and "would never return." Andrew was from Seattle and said he wanted to return home to pursue a career in marketing or advertising. There was consensus that Africa was better off without Andrew, and the sooner he left, the better.

Andrew also told us that he was in the same training group as Jesse Osmun, a twenty-something volunteer who had been arrested for having sex with young African girls from his village. He was indicted in the U.S. on federal charges that make it a felony to sexually assault children in a foreign country. This happened about the time John Jacoby arrived to be the country director, just a couple of months before my group arrived. Osmun was extradited to the U.S. and, several months later, in an email to all volunteers, John made his position clear:

"The crimes of this former volunteer are reprehensible. The Peace Corps has no tolerance for abuse of any kind, and our deepest sympathies are with all the victims involved. Peace Corps is committed to ensuring that the children affected by these crimes receive proper care and treatment. News about the case is likely to be covered in the South African press. Should you be contacted by the press or anyone in your community it is recommended that you not comment and refer any inquiries to us. It is important that we not let the act of one individual detract from the wonderful work you are doing in South Africa." Osmun eventually was sentenced in federal court in Connecticut to fifteen years in prison. Peace Corps reportedly donated $20,000 to a fund for his victims, all children under six years old.

Ironic, that South Africa, with one of the highest sexual assault rates in the world, and often described as possessing a "culture of sexual violence" that pervades society, had a Peace Corps volunteer victimize some of the most vulnerable children in the world, at the AIDS center preschool where he volunteered. This was an occasion when we were expected *not* to mirror the culture —but one of us did.

Several big events were part of training and the trainees were expected to plan, carry out or participate in them. Planning events involving hundreds of villagers was something most volunteers would be expected to do once they arrived at their sites and began planning projects with counterparts. Our first big effort was to plan and carry out a health fair directed at teaching the village children from Bundu and Matshipe about healthy eating and living. We formed committees to take on various assignments such as securing permission to use the elementary school's soccer field for the day. Jess, one of our leaders, got permission from the local inkosi for the event. The rest of us planned the activities and acquired healthy snacks like apples and pears to give to the children.

An estimated 400 children participated in the affair, which we considered a grand success. The children played tug of war, soccer, three-legged sack races (my event), water balloon tossing, and had their faces painted by Sara, from my language group. Each fun event was tied to teaching something about good health. My group, for example, showed the children the proper way to brush their teeth before they were allowed to participate in our game, for which we had prizes for winners.

Another time we split up into four groups of eight or nine and prepared "lesson plans" to present to middle school kids. My group wrote a skit in which we acted out the importance of practicing safe sex and being faithful to one's sexual partner. I portrayed a cheater who had a wife in the village and a girlfriend in the city, portrayed by Steph, my Peace Corps colleague from Utah. The "girlfriend" spread HIV by not being safe. The kids were receptive, as learners often were, to the information we offered.

11

Food Fight!

Not long after the health fair, and near the end of our training, we had to organize a celebration to honor the families who had hosted us. That meant planning the menu, assigning tasks, arranging entertainment, inviting the families, moving chairs from the big classroom to an outdoor area where food would be served, and cleaning up. The LCFs played a big role in the event and were to be in charge of the cooking. The event was going well and included Zulu dancing by both locals and Peace Corps trainees. Some of the Peace Corps women were dressed in traditional Zulu garb, provided by their village families. All five men in our group, Donovan, Greg, Dan, Christopher and I (Brant had ET'd), put on a display of Ndebele dancing we learned by watching young men from the villages, where it was a popular after school and weekend activity. We called ourselves the "American Bundu Boys." Such dancing involves periodic high kicks with one's leg, held straight out, higher than one's head. I did it many times over the months and was always surprised that I never threw out my back, fell down, kicked myself in the face or was otherwise embarrassed. I probably can't do it now since the Parkinson's has affected my balance and gait.

The afternoon was going well, but we noticed that about 400 people had come to celebrate, though only 250 or so had been invited. This is not uncommon in Zulu culture and happens all the time in villages when families plan events like pre-wedding festivities, celebrating a woman's 21st birthday *(umemulo)*, or an "unveiling," a celebration that usually comes one year after a loved one dies, and is meant to honor the departed and unveil the gravestone. Families are expected to accommodate neighbors and friends from the village who show up unexpectedly and want to be fed and wish to drink the *"umqombothi,"* the homemade Zulu beer that is a part of every celebration.

Some of us were nervous as we watched the ever-increasing crowd of people arrive, expecting to be fed. We worried the huge pots of chicken, pap and vegetables the LCFs were cooking would not be enough food. We were right. We had purchased 375 disposable plates and when those ran out and the long line remained, we retrieved plates and spoons from the trash and washed them to use again.

In my journal that night I wrote, *"It was chaotic, especially once the serving started. Not everyone got food. Ironically a lot of food went to waste when children didn't finish all the food on their plates before tossing them in the trash. Many of my fellow volunteers were upset over the lack of organization. No one seemed to be in charge; people, especially adult women, were pushing and shoving and yelling, trying to get at the last of the food."*

It was an exercise in cultural behavior, if nothing else. The next day we debriefed the event and Victor, the training manager, suggested that it would have gone a lot smoother if the food line had been set up so the food was visible to the crowd. The women had become concerned that they and their families wouldn't be served before the food ran out and they had forced themselves into the shelter where the food was located, grabbing what they could without waiting to be served. But it was American volunteers mostly who were upset. The locals, including the LCFs, took it all in stride and acted as if such behavior was ordinary. During the next year I would attend many events where food was served to large groups of people. I learned that it was common for those who had volunteered to prepare and serve food to set aside portions for themselves and their families before they served the crowd, even if it meant that not everyone got food. I witnessed similar behavior among 200 elders in Estcourt at the Golden Games, the South African equivalent of the Senior Olympics in the U.S. And at a political event in Imbabazane that included several thousand, tents and tables were knocked down when several dozen people tried to squeeze through a small opening to snatch box lunches without waiting in line.

Like many cultures, including America, in South Africa food is an important part of everyday life, of celebration, of honoring loved ones. One of my first notable experiences with food perhaps starts with the Zulu word for tomorrow: *kusasa*. It's one of the first Zulu words I learned in training. Unlike most of my fellow volunteers—who lived with families where at least one person spoke passable English—no one in my family spoke any English, so most of our communication was by sign language or acting things out.

It's Zulu custom to serve rather large portions at meals—excessive by my standards—and my Zulu family was no exception. Maria would serve me a plate of "pap," a staple of most meals made from "mealie meal" (ground corn or maize) that was almost the size of a football. With it would be chicken, the most commonly eaten meat, and servings of several vegetables—beans, spinach, beets and squash are common. Early on I learned the word *kususa* and would point at the huge plate of pap, make a chopping motion with my hand as if cutting it in half, then point to one half and say, "Kusasa…kusasa," while patting my stomach and making a small groaning sound like one would make if one were overfed.

It soon became clear that Maria knew what I was saying. But she didn't understand why I wanted to eat so little. Bhuta, who ate his pap and veggies the traditional way, with his fingers (the rest of us used spoons), always had a huge serving of pap, and ate it all, every day, though he was not as big as me. Over time, Maria began to give me smaller portions, but it was at the end of the eight weeks before she served me only as much as I could reasonably eat. Occasionally, I would find her in the kitchen as she was filling my plate. I would hold my palm up in the universal sign for stop, to keep her from overloading it. She also learned about salads when I made one for dinner one night and after that, on occasion, she would make one for me, though there was no salad dressing for it.

I recall one meal in particular where there were so many courses, ten, that I was compelled to record all the various foodstuffs as an example of a great rural South African meal. In addition to pap, the meal included chicken, squash, *"bhonchise"* (similar to baked beans), beets, salad, potatoes, rice, spinach and cabbage. I often had pap on weekends when I went to shop in Estcourt, where you can get it in restaurants, including chicken, vegetables and gravy, for twenty rand, about two dollars.

Unlike many Western countries where leftovers often are tossed, in rural South Africa food is saved for a future meal, though not always stored in a refrigerator. I saw food that was cooked, but left over and set on a counter for up to three days before someone ate it. No one got sick. I never tried that. Other times, leftovers are fed to dogs, chickens or goats. In the small cinderblock house where I lived, the electricity was so spotty that it would not support a fridge. Power was out twice for thirteen days, and once for eight. I ate a lot of peanut butter-and-jelly sandwiches, apples and a raison and nut mix I bought, along with dried peaches, pears and apricots. When I had power in the evening I often ate rice or pasta with a sauce from a package and/or canned beef, chicken or pilchards, small, sardine-like fish that come in a can with a spicy tomato sauce. Sometimes I made two servings, ate one for dinner and the balance for breakfast the next morning without its having been refrigerated. I never got sick.

Pap (sometimes pronounced "pop") is one of at least three corn-based staples that are eaten in South Africa. Pap seemed to be most popular in the northern part of the country. I described it as *a cross between cream of wheat cereal, lumpy mashed potatoes and the sticky rice one often gets in Asian restaurants.* Phutu (the "h" is silent), which is drier and more crumbly, is popular in the part of South Africa where I lived. A third staple called samp is similar to hominy or grits in the U.S. All are usually served with gravy, often with chicken. Samp was the version favored by many Xhosa, another of the tribes of South Africa. At Masiphile, where we served lunch to the children in the crèche each day—using food purchased with money provided by the Department of Social Development—the cook alternated between rice and phutu, covered with brown gravy made from soy. It was very good and I occasionally made spaghetti sauce from it at home. The gravy for the crèche kids usually included vegetables, such as carrots or potatoes, from our garden. Usually Busisisiwe, the cook, made enough for everyone to have lunch. Occasionally, she even served samp, even though she was Zulu.

According to the American Heritage Dictionary (4th edition), "samp" is of Native American origin, coming from the Narragansett word "nasàump." Since early colonial times, New Englanders have referred to cornmeal mush or cereal as "samp." Don't ask me why a word originating in early America came to be used in rural South Africa. I often had to explain to South Africans why Native Americans are called Indians, when they're not from India. But don't get me started on Columbus!

It's customary in Zulu culture to share one's food with everyone present. I committed a "faux pas" one day when I offered lunch to a worker who was at Masiphile erecting our new sign in the hot sun and was still working at lunchtime, when food was being served. I should not have offered food to one person since a group of community profilers was also there for a meeting and there wasn't enough to serve all of them. Ultimately, the worker was asked to come into the crèche classroom to eat, where he was out of sight of the group sitting in the front yard. Crisis averted, but I was more careful after that about offering lunch. Custom is to serve no one, rather than some but not others. Crèche kids excepted. I sometimes walked to the nearby tuck shop to buy cookies—what they called biscuits—to eat with tea. They came in packages of ten and rarely lasted more than one tea break, since I offered them to everyone. When I didn't buy biscuits, custom called for everyone to have three or four slices of white bread with their sugary tea. Some days, someone would bring something from home and all of us would grab a spoon and dig in, all eating from the same community bowl. For a time Philder (the "h" is silent), one of the crèche teachers, brought huge containers of baked squash, or *isijinji,* to share. Delicious! Other days we bought *igwinya*, deep fried bread rolls that are delicious, but not very healthy, from one of our neighbors. They cost a rand and a half, about 16 cents, U.S., and sometimes served with a slice of baloney.

I had another experience, not involving food, but which showed the importance in Zulu culture of not showing favoritism. Not long after I arrived in the village, all volunteers got an email from post about a program that identified hardworking, high achieving female students who could apply for scholarships to attend school in the U.S. Africa's Tomorrow (africastomorrow.org) is a program started by a former Peace Corps volunteer who had served in a different African country. He had seen the value and importance of helping female African youth to receive higher education. Its website states that the organization, "provides funding to promising female students from rural Africa in order to help them attain higher education when poverty would otherwise prevent them from continuing. We believe that educating the underprivileged is the best investment in the future and provides a catalyst for positive change throughout the world."

Unfortunately, the deadline for applying was only two weeks away. I proposed going to the two nearest high schools, within walking or easy taxi distance, to give the information to the principals so they could identify prospective candidates. I said I would even help them to complete the paperwork. Given the timeline it wasn't realistic to try to contact the other schools in distant villages since we had no phone numbers or email addresses. But Nonhlanhla insisted that we could not show favoritism and if all schools could not be contacted, then we would contact none. All had to have equal access and opportunity, or none could. It was another frustrating lesson in Zulu culture.

No explanation of Zulu food would be complete without talking about the many events that include food, such as an unveiling. I went to several of these, including the one for Busisisiwe's father-in-law, attended by both invited and uninvited guests. Like many cultures around the world, food is often a significant part of any gathering. (It's a given in South Africa that if you want good attendance at a public event your organization is sponsoring, make it known you are serving food at the end). Other family celebrations that call for lots of food and drink include celebrating a twenty-first birthday; and a celebration that calls for a groom's family to present gifts to the bride and her family, especially things that will be needed in the new couple's new household. This event also includes dressing up a goat, in a dress, to represent the new mother-in-law. And of course the traditional wedding itself, an event that commonly lasts an entire weekend or more. I attended one of the groom/bride family celebrations with Thando and Dlamini one Saturday. There were about 200 guests. It was the first time I saw a goat slaughtered and the first time I ate goat brains. That night I wrote in my journal: *"…two hours after I saw the goat cavorting in its pen—seemingly without a care in the world—I was eating its brains and liver. The killing was easier to witness than the cow I saw slaughtered last night at Zungu's neighbor's house. Four men held the goat on its back, one at each leg, while the fifth knelt at the head and slit the throat. It was over quickly."* At the groom/bride celebration Dlamini, who was driving, didn't have a single drink of alcohol, unusual in my experience when it came to Zulu men celebrating. He sat next to me while the celebration went on and explained that after the goat was killed the bladder was removed and the groom would wear it safety-pinned to the lapel of his suit for the rest of the day. Dlamini said it was "customary and traditional," but laughed and said he couldn't remember why. I Googled "goat bladders in Zulu culture" and learned there are many rituals around these organs, but I didn't learn why a groom would pin a goat bladder to his suit.

Such events are often held outside in the family compound, and involve slaughtering a cow, or cows, and a goat or two and God only knows how many chickens. I've seen and photographed the slaughter of all three, multiple times. Most Americans don't think much about going to the grocery store and buying their meat from a refrigerated case, not thinking how that meat got from the farm to the store. With a respectful and honorable nod to my vegetarian friends, I would point out that animals slaughtered in rural South African villages are treated relatively humanely and the deed is done quickly, and, for the most part, is pain-free. I'll spare the details, but done properly a cow is dead in less than a minute or so from the time the knife is pushed or tapped into the space that separates the brain from the spinal cord. This process severs the spine, and the cow doesn't feel its throat being slit to drain the blood.

Such family events almost always include serving large quantities of home-made beer, which takes several days to make, resembles chocolate milk in color, and is tasty once one gets used to it. Nonhlanhla said she would give me the recipe before I left, but circumstances of my eventual departure precluded that. Families that are relatively well off often follow the last of the home-made beer with bottled beer and, for those who stay to the end, shots of whiskey. I developed an informal policy of leaving celebrations when about half the men were intoxicated, because it usually became less fun at that point—as it would be in any culture, including ours.

The culmination of our nine weeks of training finally happened on March 22nd, definitely a highlight. My journal entry about "swearing in" reads, *"Big day…very emotional with lots of hugs, a few dignitaries, great food, many 'see ya laters,' good wishes and zillions of pictures."* For me it was the realization of a dream I had held for forty years. I was close to tears for much of the ceremony. We sang both the American and the South African national anthems. As usual, I struggled with the Afrikaner verse.

The woman who broke up with me after five years prompted my application to Peace Corps. She broke my heart but also presented me with an opportunity I likely would never have otherwise pursued. Would I trade my Peace Corps experience for a chance to turn back the clock and continue the relationship? A question I will never know the answer to, since life doesn't work that way. Not long after I got to South Africa someone told me about a website, antipodemap.com, that shows where the opposite point on Earth would be from any other point. In geography, the antipodes of any place on Earth is its antipodal point; that is, the region on the Earth's surface which is diametrically opposite to it. Two points which are antipodal to one another are connected by a straight line through the centre of the Earth. I learned that the antipode of Western Oregon is a spot in the Indian Ocean off the coast of South Africa. I literally could not have been further away from Oregon than when I was in my small Zulu village. Still, there were days when 10,000-plus miles was not far enough.

The moment we'd all been waiting for finally came. We took an oath similar to that taken by U.S. Marines, Foreign Service officers, and CIA agents to defend the Constitution, make America proud, obey the law, etc. Young Dan was chosen to say a few words in Zulu, since he had mastered the language better than anyone else. Julie, who was a speaker of Tshevenda, spoken in the northern part of South

Africa, repeated it in English. With the help of one of the LCFs Dan had written his ten-minute speech. He delivered it flawlessly. Guests included Virginia Palmer, the deputy chief of mission at the U.S. Embassy in Pretoria, who was filling in for Ambassador Donald Gips. Both she and John Jacoby offered uplifting words to the new graduates. "You will be the front line, boots on the ground" in the fight against HIV, John told us, "and you will be ambassadors of the United States."

Virginia told us that there was "about to be a policy shift" in regard to PEPFAR (President's Emergency Plan for AIDS Relief), a legacy of President George W. Bush that provided billions of dollars for AIDS work in many African countries. She said that while the U.S. would "continue to be committed to eradicating HIV/AIDS," it would also begin "deferring more" to the South African government. I've never been a fan of Bush Clan politics, but President Bush's actions were not just a nice humanitarian gesture. It was U.S. policy for many years and saved countless lives.

I sat next to Virginia at the meal that followed and regaled her with the tale of my eight tries over fifteen years to join the State Department. She was sympathetic and said I should try again. She had lived all over the world in her twenty-plus year career and spoke multiple languages, including Chinese. Later, she was able to help me find the person in the consular office in Durban, where Masiphile had applied for a grant, to check on its status. Virginia invited Doc Susan, whose housing situation in Pietermaritzburg still hadn't been sorted out, to stay in her home for a few days, since everyone agreed Susan shouldn't live at a forensic asylum. I told Susan to call me when she was settled and I would "show up with a bottle or two of wine," but I never got the invitation.

The morning of swearing in I stood outside the Bhuta Family's home drinking a cup of coffee and watched the sun rise. Beautiful, as always. I realized it was probably the last time I would see this view and experience the sounds and sights of Bundu, since my departure the next morning for my new village would be before first light. I looked at the neighbor houses across the street, and the large trees that framed a larger cell phone tower. I listened to the roosters crow, cows moo in the distance, dogs bark, goats mate, though the female didn't sound as if she was enjoying it.

That night after returning to my Bundu home, for the last time I helped Bhuta round up the five family goats that had been foraging in the village all day. There had been times in the previous two months, when Bhuta was working late and it was getting dark, that I had successfully gone alone to round up the goats (*imbuzi*, in Zulu), or chased the neighbor's cow out of our garden. Bhuta worked about twelve hours a day, six or seven days a week, chasing baboons and monkeys out of a large commercial orchard of several hectares, a mile or so from his home. It was usually dark when he left in the morning—riding a beat-up bicycle he had clearly repaired many times—and often dark when he got home. He wore knee-high rubber boots, as much to protect him from venomous snakes, I suspected, as to keep his feet dry in heavy rain. Chickens were also turned loose each day to forage, but they usually returned at night. If they didn't, each chicken owner seemed to recognize her own birds and could round them up from neighboring yards. The goats secure, I watched the sunset from Bhuta's yard for the last time. I think Venus and Jupiter were prominent in the western sky and I wondered if Cara, who lived down the street and was also interested in stars, was watching them.

12

Apartheid History:
But for Reagan and Thatcher

My two months with the Bhuta family will always be some of the most cherished memories of my fourteen months in Peace Corps. I will never forget the day I handed Maria a pair of reading glasses, purchased for a dollar back home, and told her to try them on. Flabbergasted is the only word that does justice, and only barely, to her reaction. I suspect it had been years since she had been able to read or see words on pages or figures clearly in pictures. Once her amazement subsided, she made a beeline for a nearby cabinet and took out a small book of prayers, opened to what might have been a favorite page, and read. She began to cry. I let her keep the glasses—I had brought several pairs, in anticipation of just such an occasion—but could never have predicted such a stunning moment, such a small yet impactful event. It's one of the highlights of my service. She in turn gave me a traditional Ndebele hand-made grass mat—also made by Zulus—that are both beautiful and functional. (Mdu's mother also made them and told me it takes about three days, working several hours a day, to complete one, using a home-made loom. They sell for one hundred rand, about $10). Maria's mat adorns the coffee table in my living room. A few months after my return to America I sent Maria another pair of glasses and a beautiful framed watercolor rendering of a Zulu prayer done by my artist daughter, Megan. The prayer, in English, hung in Maria's kitchen. I wrote it down one day and asked Minky, my LCF, to translate it into Zulu (which is similar to Ndebele, Maria's first language), which Megan reproduced, in Zulu. Maria now has versions in both languages. Since Maria didn't have a mailing address, I couldn't have delivered the gift without the help of my volunteer colleague, Lilly, whose two-year assignment was in Bundu, where she lived next door to the Bhuta family.

I never learned Bhuta's first name. He was about seventy to Maria's sixty-four and though he was a black South African and a Zulu, his first language, the only language he spoke fluently, was Afrikaans, the Dutch-like language developed by the whites. The language that under apartheid black South Africans of a certain era were forced to learn, while giving up the language of their heritage.

The Bantu Education Act of 1953 is described on Wikipedia as "a pillar of the apartheid concept." The legislation was intended to separate black South Africans from the comparatively well-resourced education system for whites. Authored by Dr. H. F. Verwoerd (then Minister of Native Affairs, and later Prime Minister), it established a Black Education Department in the Division of Native Affairs, the agency charged with developing a curriculum that suited the "nature and requirements of the black people." African students—later to be called learners—were to be educated in ways that were "appropriate for their culture." There was no consultation with the effected blacks about this new plan. All the definitions of culture, appropriate education content and levels, all the decisions about purpose and outcomes of the system were controlled by the apartheid government. Its stated aim was to prevent Africans from receiving an education that would lead them to "aspire to positions they wouldn't be allowed to hold in society," Wikipedia states. Instead black Africans were to receive an education designed to provide them with skills to serve their own people in the "homelands" or to work in manual labor jobs under white control.

White Afrikaners believed they were doing blacks a favor by relegating them to second class status. I can't imagine anything more condescending. The legislation was condemned by black South Africans and most of the rest of the world as inferior from the time of its introduction. This cornerstone of apartheid ideology "wreaked havoc on the education of black people in South Africa, and deprived and disadvantaged millions for decades. Its devastating personal, political and economic effects continue to be felt and wrestled with today," according to Wikipedia.

Bantu education was a companion program to the one that ordered millions of blacks to relocate from white areas to "homelands," similar to reservations the American government sent some Native Americans to in the 1800s.

"African farm laborers made up the largest number of forcibly removed people, mainly pushed out of their jobs by mechanization of agriculture," according to sahistory.org. "While this process has happened in many other countries, in South Africa these rural residents were not permitted to move to towns to find new jobs. Instead, they were segregated into desperately poor and overcrowded rural areas where there usually were no job prospects.

"Removals were an essential tool of the apartheid government's Bantustan (or homeland) policy aimed at stripping all black Africans of any political rights as well as their citizenship in South Africa. Hundreds of thousands of Africans were moved to resettlement camps in the Bantustans with no services or work," according to sahistory.org.

In the years after apartheid became official policy, blacks were permitted to be in cities as long as they worked for whites. The policy contributed to the weakness of the black South African family—a legacy of apartheid when the law forced adults to seek work far from home, going for weeks or months at a time without seeing their children, so they could earn money to send home to their families. This legacy haunts black South Africa to this day. I met many families where one parent worked in Durban or Joburg or Pretoria and came home only occasionally.

The Afrikaner belief that whites in early South African history were meant to rule blacks stemmed from an interpretation of verses in the Old Testament that implied such actions were directions from God. In his novel *The Covenant*, American novelist James Michener, known for his fictional but historically accurate books, describes the "covenant," or agreement between God and the early Afrikaners, who likened themselves to the biblical Israelites, who also saw themselves as God's chosen people. Eventually, in the early twentieth century, the Afrikaners institutionalized their beliefs about racial purity, separatism and white supremacy into apartheid. Ironically, many of those early Dutch settlers who left Europe did so to escape religious persecution.

My reading of South African history suggests that one significant reason apartheid lasted as long as it did was that in the 1980s the United States under President Ronald Reagan and England under Prime Minister Margaret Thatcher supported the white apartheid-minded government, by refusing to support sanctions against South Africa that most of the civilized world endorsed. Eventually, the U.S. and England were dragged into the moving tide of anti-apartheid culture, but it took many more years for England and the U.S. to join the right side of history.

Bhuta's home had running water—much of the time—but other times the water would stop for up to five days. When the water was running we would survive on what had been collected in our fourteen or so five-gallon buckets, about seventy gallons, to be used when the water stopped for all cooking, cleaning, drinking, bathing and laundry. Bathing is done via a "bucket bath" and, if you were careful, you could do it with less than two gallons. When I got to Goodhome, the village where I would live for a year, I quickly learned that when I had to walk 300 yards for water and carry the forty-pound bucket back, after cranking the pump handle 135 times, I never wanted to waste water.

Not all my volunteer colleagues had such good experiences in their homes. Some were underfed at times, the opposite of my experience. Some lived in homes where alcohol abuse and all that goes with it was a prominent dynamic in the family. It's likely that some lived in homes where adults weren't always faithful to their partners. Some volunteers, on the other hand, lived in homes where they developed close relationships with everyone, especially the children of the family, not to mention the dogs named Gary.

I met many of Bhuta and Maria's neighbors, and their children, who were always curious about the white man—*umlungu*, in Zulu—when I lived in their village. They had questions about white culture, about America, about my own family, and about what Brad Pitt, Beyoncé, Paris Hilton and Mitt Romney were really like. A child once asked a fellow volunteer if it was true that "Americans take their animals to a doctor?" Some children were shy, but most were friendly and talkative. One afternoon Selena, a girl about sixteen, saw me sitting on the front porch and came into the yard to ask if needed help learning Zulu. I said sure and we spent an hour practicing the language. I told her she was welcome to come by anytime to help me. I never talked to her again, though she always waved when she walked by. A few days later, on St. Patrick's Day, three girls, Andile and Surprise, who were twelve, and Duduzile, nine, stopped by to visit. They told me they lived with my Peace Corps colleague, Kristen, a couple of streets over, and said that her African name was Nobuhle, which means "beautiful" in Zulu. I gave them a deck of cards to play with, which entertained them until they decided to pick guavas from the front yard tree. That night I wrote in my journal: *"St. Patrick's Day and I have no green beer and no one to not drink it with."*

One of the highlights of our nine weeks in Bundu was the Saturday afternoon when all Bundu volunteers, about twenty of us, were invited to attend the ceremony and celebration that happens when a girl turns fifteen. We were told a goat would be killed and served in our honor. The ceremony took place in the compound that was right next to Bhuta's place and at its height there must have been more than 200 people there. The Zulu beer flowed freely and I sampled it for the first time, but only a couple of sips from the community beer pitcher. There were about eight girls celebrating their coming of age, or *umhlonyana* (oom-sh-lone-YAWN-a). They wore traditional garb and danced for their families and everyone else. They were topless, which would of course be frowned upon in Western cultures like ours, but is natural in Zulu and Ndebele culture. I took pictures. The father who was hosting the gathering led me through a crowd of onlookers to ensure I had a good view from the front row. When I told him I might be arrested in America for taking photos of topless fifteen-year-old girls he laughed and didn't understand. When I posted a couple of pictures on Facebook I was careful to explain that "in Western culture female breasts are sexual objects, while in many African cultures breasts are merely tools for feeding babies or holding cell phones in place." Still, there were female SA25 colleagues who I think came to believe, incorrectly, that I was obsessed with cleavage, when, a few months later I posted a picture of a young woman storing her cell phone in her bra. I'd never seen that in America, though my daughter, Megan, told me it was common.

This was also the first time some of us got to try the local dance that eventually we would perform in front of our village friends and families at the thank you event for our hosts. Donovan, as always, was front and center, while I held back at first. I was busy holding a small baby someone plopped into my arms. The parents left and didn't return for some time. I feared I might have a bedmate that night. The party went on into the wee hours of Sunday morning. Between that and the neighbor on the other side, who played '70s soft rock tunes loudly at all hours, I didn't get much sleep that night. It was about ninety degrees (F) and humid. Some nights I didn't truly sleep until the temperature dropped into the low eighties, which wasn't until three or four in the morning—when the roosters also started crowing.

I left the party about seven, mostly to get away from "Bobo," a man from the neighborhood who was more annoying than most intoxicated people. In the fourteen months I lived in rural South Africa I dealt with many intoxicated people, mostly men, and many panhandlers. None was ever obnoxious or threatening, or made me fearful. One morning a few months later I was walking along the main tar road to a church service to which I'd been invited and encountered a drunken woman who had fallen into the roadway. I pulled her back to the sidewalk and encouraged her to be careful. Another problem associated with drinking too much alcohol is the cultural quirk that makes it okay for rural black men to urinate in public places. I observed this hundreds of times and no one ever seemed the least bit perturbed, though someone told me it was illegal. I saw women do this only twice and both times they were much more discreet than the men.

Another cultural phenomenon I never found an explanation for was why Zulu men frequently grab their crotches, often while walking down the street. Our male cultural facilitators were unable to explain it, nor could my female colleagues at Masiphile. They thought it was funny that I would ask, and odd when I told them that most American women would find it crude, or offensive if such an act was also accompanied by sexually suggestive remarks. The closest I ever came to an explanation was in an essay by Noah Brand (goodmenproject.com), a white Portlander who writes about men's issues: "Enough with the jokes about how weird and gross it is. The equipment shifts around, it changes shape and size, it chafes, and it is very sensitive. When it gets uncomfortable, it gets very uncomfortable indeed, so cut us a little slack, could you?" I guess that could apply to both Zulus and whites.

Zulu men sometimes also hold hands or link arms while walking down the street. There's nothing sexual about it. The most masculine of men do it. Just part of their culture. Zulu men took me by the hand a time or two to lead me someplace—like a parent might do with a child—and thought nothing of it.

Eventually, our nine weeks in Bundu or Matshipe ended and it was time for the event we'd been training for and dreaming about for many months: departure to the villages where we would spend the next two years. The next morning the Peace Corps van was picking me up about five for the long ride to Southwestern KwaZulu-Natal. At the pink stucco home of Bhuta, Maria and Siyabonga, we had said our good-byes the night before and all went to bed at the usual time, about nine.

I was up before anyone else, anxious to get on to the next adventure, but sad to leave the people who had so generously welcomed me into their family. I couldn't get the key to open the gate between the yard and the street. I finally went back to the front door and tossed the key through the "burglar bars" common in all South African homes, both black and white. I tossed my bags over the fence and climbed over after them, managing not to impale myself on the sharp metal spears that lined the top of the fence—an alternative to the razor wire common at so many homes. South Africa has one of the highest crime rates in the world and residents of all races are quite security conscious.

Assembled at Khosanna for the last time, we said our good-byes to one another, took lots of pictures, exchanged hugs, and loaded our bags into kombis, and trailers Peace Corps had rented for the occasion. We dropped Ann from Long Beach, CA off in Ladysmith; Andrea, Rachel, and Christopher and Emily, in Bergville; then Peggie in Winterton, the town where many of us would go to for those Friday night volunteer potlucks. (Andrea's placement in Bergville shortly failed, through no fault of hers, and she moved to Winterton to join Peggie at her organization, Isibani. Eventually Andrea landed in Limpopo Province). Finally, there was no one left but me. Eleven hours after we left Bundu, "AB", the Peace Corps driver, dropped me and my luggage in front of the Nestle plant in downtown Estcourt. Nonhlanhla had called my cell phone and told us they had to finish some errands before meeting me. After I'd sat on the curb for half an hour in front of Nestle, Nonhlanhla, Thando and Dlamini finally arrived in a small, but sporty blue SUV called a Daihatsu Terios, a model I'd never seen in the U.S. (I would ride in that car many times, in true South African fashion, with as many as eight other people, though it was designed to hold no more than four).

I'd spent some of the wait time talking with an Indian man named Sanjay, who was on his dinner break from the plant. His wife would arrive soon with his meal in a paper sack. I told him what I was doing there and he said he'd worked at Nestle twenty years. He said Estcourt was "a good place to live," but also warned me to "watch out." He didn't say what I should watch out for, but on my first full day as a Peace Corps volunteer, I experienced one of the most bizarre evenings of my life.

13

"My Sister Stole the Keys and Ran Away to Durban"

As we headed for the village, a twenty-five-kilometer, thirty-minute drive from Estcourt (faster by taxi), Nonhlanhla called Sipho (SEE-po) to tell him we were on the way. No answer. She tried several more times, but never reached him. We were parked on the road in front of his house where we could see, beyond the tall fence with razor wire on top, that the lights were on and people were moving about. *"And then it got weird,"* I later wrote in my journal. While I watched these mysterious developments from the rear seat, Nonhlanhla and Dlamini conversed in Zulu. I couldn't understand them, but finally they called Councilor Mkhize to ask his assistance. He arrived shortly, with two bodyguards, and tried to negotiate a solution. Sipho came out of the house twice and walked back and forth in the front yard, but ignored the people hollering at him, and the cars parked beyond his gate.

After about forty-five minutes, Sipho walked down the driveway to the gate. A short conversation ensued between him, Nonlanhla and Mkhize. Finally, they returned to Dlamini's car and Sipho went back to his house. Nonhlanhla said there was "a challenge" with the gate. Sipho's sister had taken the only key and gone to Durban, 150 miles away. I knew this not to be true, since two weeks earlier I had spent

123

four days at the house and Sipho and I each had our own set of keys. Even if it were true, he could have told us of the problem in one of the phone calls he refused to answer. Or the lock could have been cut off with bolt cutters and easily replaced the next day. I had such a lock in my luggage. They decided that my first night would be in a bed and breakfast back in Estcourt, the Thyme and Again, and we would sort it out the next day. We retraced our steps to town, they helped me check in, and Dlamini paid 500 rand, about $60, breakfast included, with a credit card. It was 9 p.m.

Eventually, Nonhlanhla told me that Sipho had changed his mind about hosting me but didn't have the nerve to tell her. It wouldn't be the only time I saw what psychologists might have said was passive-aggressive behavior. What would be diagnosable back home was just part of the culture in black South Africa. I never spoke to Sipho again, though I did see him drive by a couple of times, while seeming to ignore me. I thought of such people as "PAPs"—passive-aggressive procrastinators—because of their annoying behaviors. I also came to accept such behavior—and occasionally found it endearing—because it was a part of the culture. My own theory about Sipho's bizarre behavior has always been that he finally accepted what I had told him several times during the pre-placement visit—I couldn't get him a job. Once he believed that, he no longer had interest in hosting me.

Nonhlanhla told me she would call me in the morning and let me know when someone would pick me up. At breakfast in the dining room, who should be there eating but AB, the driver who had dropped me off the night before. I explained what had happened and he laughed, not surprised that there had been a glitch on my first day. I came to learn that such glitches, especially around housing issues, were common. Many of my fellow 25ers also had housing issues, some multiple times. I helped AB hook up the cargo trailer to the Peace Corps van, and took a bag of belongings that Rachel had accidentally left behind, promising to return it to her.

I no sooner saw AB off when Nonhlanhla called to tell me that her younger sister, Hlengiwe (shlen-GEE-way), whom I would come to know well, would meet me in front of the B&B and take me to her apartment across from the Nestle plant where she worked from four to midnight. She lived with her twelve-year-old daughter, Clemusa, and her toddler son, Khonke (CONE-kay). There was no man in the picture. Shortly, Nonhlanhla arrived and the five of us spent the rest of the day talking and playing Monopoly in Hlengiwe's tiny apartment. At one point Clemusa—who often went by Musa for short—took me on a walk around downtown Estcourt. She spoke English well and we talked about school, her interests and her life there.

I slept that night in Hlengiwe's large bed, one that ordinarily accommodated her and her children. She insisted that as a guest I get the only bed. She and her kids and Nonhlanhla slept on spare mattresses on the "living room" floor, which was separated from the bedroom by a curtain. The next day she made breakfast for all of us, pap with chicken and gravy, while Nonhlanhla was on the phone, trying to find a place for me to live. I sent a text message to my Peace Corps supervisor, Matseke, one of the associate Peace Corps directors, to let him know of my circumstances. I told him I wasn't worried, and that I was certain it would all work out. By the end of the day Nonhlanhla had not solved my housing problem, so we decided I would stay at her home in the village of Sobabili ("the two of us" in Zulu) until a more permanent solution could be found. This violated Peace Corps policy, which says a volunteer can't live with a supervisor, but we understood it was an emergency and hopefully of short duration.

My night at Nonhlanhla's home turned into two weeks, during which she arranged for her friend the high school principal, Tito Zungu, to talk with me about the possibility of staying in one of the extra structures at his family compound in Goodhome. We agreed it was a workable solution and arranged for me to visit his place the next day so I could see my possible new digs before agreeing to stay there.

The place he offered was a small, gray cinderblock house, later painted pink, of about 400 square feet. There were two decent-sized bedrooms, both off a larger kitchen/living area. No bathroom. It was one of the so-called rural development houses, 700,000 of which had been built by the South African government for families all over the provinces. For those who had been living in rondavels or mud huts, the block houses were a nice step up. For Mr. Zungu, who already had a nice house, it became a building in which others would live.

After I'd been there a couple of months he and I were talking about my Peace Corps service. He was amazed to know that when I returned to the U.S., the government would not just give me a house for free. The idea that I would have to borrow *at least* a million rand (about $100,000) to buy a house not much bigger than the one I was living in was incomprehensible to him. I explained that though there were government programs that sometimes helped those with lower incomes, they didn't just give one a house. He was amazed to learn that for me to buy even a modest home I would have to come up with a couple hundred thousand rand for a down payment, then borrow another 800,000 rand from a bank or lending company and pay it back, with interest, over twenty or thirty years. Of course, in the U.S. it would be a house with reliable power and a bathroom with a toilet and shower. No free house was a concept to which he couldn't relate.

I learned I would share the house with one of his nephews, Sendile, a twenty-eight-year-old police officer in the South African Police Services. His post was about sixty kilometers away, in Weenan, and he generally came home, by taxi, every other weekend. He stayed in the second bedroom in the cinderblock house, which violated a Peace Corps policy that mandates volunteers stay in private space separate from family quarters, or have a separate private entrance.

But by then I'd stayed in five different places in less than a month—Sipho's, the bed and breakfast, Hlengiwe's apartment, Nonhlanhla's home and, finally, with Zungu's family. I chose not to make an issue of it since I could see that Nonhlanhla was putting so much energy into accommodating me in difficult circumstances and, though my housing always felt a little tenuous, for as long as I was there, I never regretted my decision to accept what was offered. Other volunteers had more challenging housing issues. Sendile was a kind, thoughtful, generous, usually quiet, intelligent man. He spent much of his weekends at home studying to take tests to get promoted. We got along well. Even after those nights his girlfriend stayed over and the loud music they played didn't block certain sounds from their quiet neighbor's sensitive ears. It didn't help that the more-or-less hollow walls in cinderblock houses stopped three feet short of the ceiling/roof, leaving plenty of room for rafter mice, spiders, sounds and just about anything else to pass back and forth between the two bedrooms. He didn't match the reputation that many people had of the South African Police Services, that many officers were corrupt and incompetent.

I enjoyed my two weeks at Nonhlanhla's, as it gave me an opportunity to observe culture in a setting different from where I would head for the foreseeable future. And at times it was humorous. After my first night Nonhlanhla gave me the standard plastic tub for bathing. This would be my first bucket bath, although I had seen it demonstrated in PST by one of the male LCFs. In Bundu the Bhuta family had an old claw-foot tub one could put a small amount of water into; and at Sipho's house there was a curtained outdoor shower, fed by the Jojo, a huge tank that gathered rainwater. Nonhlanhla pointed to the kitchen, indicating that's where the water was. I thought she was saying that's where I should bathe, which seemed odd so I said, "In the kitchen?"

"Yebo," she said, using the Zulu word for yes, then disappeared into her bedroom. I put a few inches of water in the tub, stripped down to my shorts, and began to wash. Suddenly, Nonhlanhla reappeared, saw me nearly naked on her kitchen floor and screamed, covering her mouth with a hand. She quickly retreated and I finished washing and put my clothes back on. Turned out she hadn't really understood what I had asked when she answered "yes." Bathing was to be done in the privacy of one's room.

One night a man about sixty stopped by unexpectedly. He was blind in one eye and walked with a pronounced limp. She introduced him as her "uncle," a term I later learned is often used to describe older male acquaintances who aren't necessarily related biologically. I was also called "uncle" a time or two (and *bwana*, which is Swahili for master or boss). The man had dinner with us, watched a soccer game on television, then slept in the empty bedroom. He had brought nothing with him—no change of clothes, no toothbrush. Later, Nonhlanhla described him as "a little mentally retarded," perhaps from the childhood accident that had claimed one of his eyes. The next morning I fixed breakfast—scrambled eggs, sliced tomatoes, white bread and tea for the three of us—and our guest left. I never saw him again. I gave the leftover food scraps to the two scrawny dogs next door, one of whom was nursing a litter of pups. Nonhlanhla claimed she had never before made scrambled eggs and asked me to teach her.

Another day Nonhlanhla took me on a quarter-mile walk down the main dirt road in Sobabili to meet the induna, the executive assistant to Sobabili's inkosi, or chief. I understood none of the conversation between Nonhlanhla and the induna, which was all in Zulu. We returned to Nonhlanhla's house only to discover that I had inadvertently locked the keys in the house. Nonhlanhla sent me next door to visit with her neighbor while she searched the neighborhood for a toddler-sized human small enough to squeeze through the burglar bars on the window, and old enough to understand how to open the locked door from the inside. After a short time: mission accomplished! I didn't witness the break-in since I was next door, but it sounded humorous.

The next day, when I returned from a trip to Estcourt to buy groceries for Nonhlanhla, I conversed with the twenty-ish taxi driver, who spoke passable English. He asked me if I was from Zimbabwe, since, apparently, many whites in South Africa are from there. He was amazed to hear I was American and there for two years as a volunteer, and that I didn't have a wife. "Why not?" he asked.

I laughed and said, "Because I can take care of myself." We talked about how some men have multiple wives and I mentioned that South African President Jacob Zuma had five wives, but that in the U.S. it's illegal for a man to have more than one spouse at a time.

"Even your president?" he asked.

"Even President Obama is allowed only one wife," I told him. He found it hard to believe.

The first time I returned to Nonhlanhla's home after moving to Zungu's compound, she and Hlengiwe invited me to a family event honoring her ancestors, for whom they had built a small alter in the bedroom I had occupied. Next to the alter: ten gallons of homemade beer. I also noticed there had been some outdoor improvements, including mending the fence. It was a Sunday and I walked from Goodhome using the new pedestrian footbridge, which took an hour on a day it was sunny and reasonably warm, but breezy. That night I wrote in my journal, and on Facebook: *"Got very windy today here in the foothills of The Drakensburg, which means much dust since it hasn't rained for more than a week. If I ever start a rock band I think I will name it Ubiquitous Dust. Or maybe I'll change my name to that when I go home in a couple of years, and make up an interesting, amazing, outrageous, and completely bogus story about how I got that name. Something to do with a knife fight, perhaps! And I would have the prominent scar on my forehead to back up my story. Later, maybe, I would confess that the scar was actually the result of walking into a barbed-wire fence one weekend at Nonhlanhla's, only coincidentally after drinking home-made African beer!"*

14

Dancing with Gogos

March 26, 2012: *"My first full day at Masiphile,"* I wrote in my journal that night. *"I spent the morning observing, and participating in training about HIV and AIDS for Masiphile's home-based care volunteers. The first phone call of the day – to Nonhlanhla's cell phone, since Masiphile doesn't have phone service—was from a volunteer who reported that her sister was killed last night when she was struck by lightning during the 5 p.m. storm we all experienced."*

The training opened with *"singing and prayers long enough and loud enough to rival some of the long-winded preachers I've known back home,"* I wrote. This is the way most mornings started. Midway through the singing a man walked by outside, swinging a machete, perhaps on his way to harvest grass, and joined in the merriment, singing along. There were about twenty-five volunteers, all female except one man, Innocent. One of the trainers, an experienced volunteer, talked about the importance of using condoms to prevent sharing infection. As she spoke, she moved her hand back and forth, fingers curled, in the nearly universal gesture for male masturbation. I presumed it was inadvertent, more like a nervous tic than a conscious effort to demonstrate an alternative to condom use. One of the trainees was a girl about fifteen, there with her mother. We broke into small groups, as in Peace Corps training, and discussed ways in which young people could effectively be taught about the importance of protecting themselves from HIV. My group "elected" me to present our findings to the rest of the group when we reassembled. I did so in English and everyone seemed to understand.

At the end of the day Nonhlanhla and I got a ride back to Sobabili from Linda (pronounced LEEN-da), husband of one of the volunteers. They thought it was funny when I told them "linda" is a Spanish word for pretty and is a common American name for girls. Two days later, after a wait of ninety minutes, we took a taxi home. We had learned, between the village and the city, Estcourt, police had set up roadblocks to check taxis for licenses, working lights and turn signals and to ensure taxis weren't overloaded. Nonhlanhla explained there were fewer taxis on the road because many drivers had been warned by phone about the checks and, if they were operating illegally, the drivers took their taxis out of service for the rest of the day to avoid being cited. I estimated that thirty full taxis passed us by before one with enough room for two more finally stopped for us. Some of those didn't stop because we signaled we were going to Sobabili and they were headed to other villages. Every village had a hand signal associated with it so taxis wouldn't waste time stopping for people going elsewhere.

It was while we were waiting for a kombi that Nonhlanhla told me I was the first white person *ever* to have lived in this area of 60,000 people. *"No wonder people are always staring at me,"* I wrote in my journal that night. *"Now I know how black people in white bread Eugene and parts of Portland feel."* There were white people in Estcourt, but not many.

It was also a memorable day for another reason: it was my first time participating in the Luncheon Club, our weekly group for seniors, or elders. Informally they were known as "The Gogos," or the gogo group. Gogo is the Zulu word for grandmother. This was a group of about a dozen, mainly women 60-75 years old. They met at Masiphile to socialize, talk about important issues, and, when the weather was decent, do exercises or play games outside to get in shape for the upcoming senior Golden Games. Sometimes they danced and I would join them; they didn't care that I wasn't a very good dancer! "Dancing with gogos" became one of my favorite activities at Masiphile. They were a talented group, and many of them handmade mats, purses, bags, cell phone holders and hats to sell to help support their families. One of my projects eventually became finding a way to help the gogos market their products via a "fair trade" store in Springfield, Oregon, a neighboring town of Eugene

A few months after my arrival, after the gogos had been practicing for months, the day finally arrived for the regional competition in Estcourt where they would compete against elders from other villages in our area. Nonhlanhla had said that the bus was supposed to pick us up about 8:30, but probably wouldn't come until 9:30 or ten. This didn't surprise me, since everything was always late. I figured I would get there at the usual time, 7:45. The gogos started to arrive at Masiphile about 8:30. By ten everyone was there—but no bus. At about 11:35, almost four hours after I got there, I asked Welile (Wel-LEE-lay), who was sitting behind the building chatting in the sun with Phila, "How long until we accept that the bus isn't going to come and give up?" Welile laughed and said, "I knew yesterday the bus wouldn't come. The Department of Sport and Recreation said it was too far to come to pick up our seniors." I was dumbfounded.

I had many questions, such as, why did we let twenty-five people show up and stand around for three or four hours if we knew the bus wasn't coming? But, I didn't say anything. Clearly, cultural considerations were at play here and I didn't know how or if I should say more. I had decided I could be more productive by walking to the library to see if I could access the Internet on the village Wi-Fi. Five minutes later, at 11:42, the bus came. Welile had been wrong. We boarded the bus, went to town, had a great time and our elders did well, as they always do. The moral of the story: don't give up after four hours, because in five more minutes the solution might magically appear!

An incident at the Golden Games, which featured a couple hundred competitors, also confirmed my earlier thinking about feeding large groups. Just as had happened at the end of training, when the box lunches with chicken were served at the games, there was mass chaos as hundreds of senior citizens made a run on the dining building. I was a senior, but not a competitor so I rationalized that I didn't deserve a free lunch. Besides, I didn't want to have to elbow old people aside for a piece of chicken. I went hungry until I got home and made a peanut butter and jelly sandwich, a staple of my diet when the power was out, which was about forty percent of the time.

The next week's Luncheon Club meeting was set in a circle of chairs in the grass out front and Nonhlanhla facilitated a discussion about how the grannies could effectively promote safe sex, especially condom use, in their families. I listened until the end when I asked Nonhlanhla if she would translate a few words for me. I told the gogos I was very impressed with their discussion, adding, "If I tried to talk about condom use in front of my grandmother back in the U.S., she would have fainted and fallen over." They all laughed. I miss them.

A few days later Nonhlanhla announced it was time to meet the inkosi, or chief. During my four-day pre-placement visit I had met with the induna when he came to my rondavel at Sipho's. Nonhlanhla introduced him as Mthintwo Shadrach Khumalo, an older man who, she later told me, was wealthy by local standards because he owned a lot of property, including his own forest. There are a few people in Oregon who are also considered wealthy because they own their own forests. All appeared impressed when I pointed out that Shadrach is a character from the Old Testament. According to the Book of Daniel, Shadrach survived being thrown into a fiery furnace—along with his Jewish friends Meshach and Abednego—by the Babylonian king. All were saved due to divine intervention. Mthintwo had a sense of humor and laughed when he told Nonhlanhla that she should have given me one of his Zulu names, instead of the name Musa. The gathering went well and he approved a meeting with the inkosi.

When we arrived at the home of the inkosi, Nobentungwa – (no-ben-TUNE-gwa) a matronly woman in her fifties—she was busy leading a prayer gathering of women in a rondavel-like structure that was shorter than most and used only for spiritual activities. One had to stoop to enter. There had been a similar one at Sipho's family compound. Inside, about ten women were sitting cross-legged on the dirt floor. Nonhlanhla and I were directed to enter Nobentungwa's house, remove our shoes, and wait in the living room for her to complete her duties. We waited about thirty minutes, watching television, thanks to a satellite dish. The TV hung high in a corner and "China Beach," one of my favorite shows from the 80s—about doctors and nurses in battle during the Vietnam War—was showing. Finally, the chief came through the front door and, without saying a word or acknowledging us in any way, walked past us and into another room.

A few minutes later she reappeared, having changed from her ceremonial garb to a nice dress. She greeted Nonhlanhla as an old friend and they spoke for several minutes in Zulu. Nonhlanhla told her about Peace Corps and some of the projects I might do, then introduced me to Nobentungwa. I responded in the greeting I had been practicing for days: "Ngiyajabula ukukukwaze," which means "I am pleased to meet you." I continued in English, saying, "I hope to help your community a great deal while I am here." She and Nonhlanhla spoke for another couple of minutes and then we left. I never saw the inkosi again. Following the correct protocol when I met with the induna, and the chief, though formal and brief, was important.

My experience and those of most volunteers were probably similar and went well. But not everyone's did. When Christopher and Emily met the inkosi in their village Chris (or was it Rachel? My notes aren't clear), told him he had been a college student studying political science. The inkosi didn't understand and concluded, incorrectly, that Christopher was there in a political role, to challenge his authority. The inkosi, apparently feeling threatened, reacted with anger, gesticulating and ordering the couple to get out of his village. The person who brought them intervened and explained that Chris and Emily had no desire to oppose the inkosi politically and were there only to help. When Julie, who was far north in Limpopo Province, went to meet the inkosi in her village he was nowhere to be found. However, eventually, they found him passed out in a nearby field, intoxicated. It was a brief meeting.

A few days later Nonhlanhla took me to my first meeting of the Imbabazane Local AIDS Council, part of a provincial program that in turn coordinated with the national program, to track the various activities that address the

HIV/AIDS crisis. The local AIDS council included representatives of health organizations, traditional healers, the "women's sector," the "men's sector," youth, the disabled, persons living with HIV/AIDS, and government. The "sectors" represented issues specific to men and women.

This was the first time I met the mayor, a tall, sharply dressed, attractive woman in her fifties, who led the meeting. It was also the first time I saw how close rural South Africans are to their cell phones. The mayor stood in front of the large council chamber, at a podium, before about fifty people, and was only fifteen minutes into her speech when her cell phone rang. She stopped in the middle of a sentence, retrieved her phone from her purse, and had a conversation. After a minute or so she finished her phone call and resumed the meeting. Before it was over, several other people had calls and either answered them, or quickly left the room to take the call. I had put my phone on vibrate so it wouldn't disrupt the meeting, but others rarely did that.

South Africa and other largely rural countries on the continent went from having no technology with which to communicate to suddenly having cell phones, missing the landline era. Businesses and homes in cities had regular phone service, but rarely was it found in rural areas until cell phones came along. I learned early: Don't get between South Africans and their cell phones! I observed that no matter how poor someone was, most seemed to have found a way to afford a cell phone. This was possible in part because most cell service in rural areas was based on buying "airtime" in small increments from ten to fifty rand (about $5.00, U.S.) at a time. There is no monthly bill like there is in the U.S. If you ran out of minutes on your phone, you were unable to communicate until you scrounged up a few rand to buy a voucher at the nearest tuck shop, enter the PIN and be back in business. Many people had two phones – one for each major carrier (Vodacom and MTN) so that if weather or some other misfortune disrupted one system, you had a phone that would work in the other. And if you had a phone for work, you might have three phones. I saw several people who did.

15

*The Community Integration Period,
or 'Lockdown'*

When I arrived in the village for the pre-placement visit I began gathering information for the community needs assessment, a process that enables new volunteers to get to know their villages, neighbors, organizations, and community needs. This leads to joint decisions, made by the volunteers and the organizations they work with, about what projects the volunteer will undertake. Peace Corps calls this the "community integration period." Cynical volunteers call it "lockdown" because you're not supposed to leave the village during the first ninety days at your new site, except to go to your "shopping town" to reload on groceries and supplies. After the ninety days came IST—Intermediate Service Training—where we all met in Pretoria to debrief our first three months, share war stories, and catch up with friends we'd not seen since our swearing in.

My CNA was sixteen single-spaced pages. Might have had something to do with being a writer. I had no idea how it would compare to those of my fellow volunteers. Nonhlanhla declared it "brilliant" when she read it, but I doubted its brilliance. I thought I had pretty high standards as a writer and declared it decent, but not brilliant.

Much of the information in my report came from the municipality's five-year (2012-2016) planning document.

And I never missed an opportunity to ask people about their lives and experiences, and what they thought their community needed most. The conversations reminded me of my early days as a newspaper reporter.

Imbabazane is a rural community, with no cities or townships (a township is bigger than a village, but smaller than a city). The municipality has thirty-two identified villages, as well as six "traditional tribal authorities." Villages have names like Zwelisha, Loksloy, Bhekuzulu, Nyosini, Mahlutshini, Shayamoya, Roosdale, Mandabeni and Hlathikhulu. Most names were clearly Zulu in origin, but Dutch, Roosdale, Loksloy and Goodhome sounded like they may have been English, Afrikaner or Dutch in origin.

The government authors of the plan were honest in their assessment: "The municipality, like others in the country, is faced with a variety of challenges, including inadequate access to basic services, inadequate transport system, high levels of illiteracy, poverty, unemployment, the HIV/AIDS epidemic, and insufficient resources for infrastructure development." This document identified education and health, economic development, and infrastructure development and basic service delivery as its highest priorities for the next five years.

The municipality had 140,700 people—roughly the same population as Eugene, my home town, and about 140,500 of those are black. Two hundred are "Coloured," which is not necessarily a derogatory term in South Africa, as it is in the U.S., but refers to those who are of "mixed race" descent, or "a heterogeneous ethnic group whose members possess ancestry from Europe and various Khoisan and Bantu tribes of Southern Africa," according to Wikipedia. The municipality also included a few whites, none of whom, but me, seemed to live in my collection of eighteen or so villages that made up the southern part of the municipality. The remaining villages were spread out, it appeared, on the distant side of Imbabazane to the north. My colleague Kristin, the engineer from Albuquerque, lived in one of those villages. She told me how to find the five-year plan online and used that information in her CNA, too. Thankfully, it was in English. (In the apartheid era people were formally classified with one of four labels: White, Black, Coloured or Indian).

Other issues, identified by the plan at the district level (many municipalities make up a district), were orphans and vulnerable children, youth and children in trouble with the law, "youth exposed to trauma," abused women and children, substance abuse, "widows, divorced and disabled rural women," the indigent and the homeless, "granny- and child-headed households," and "unskilled, unemployed and retrenched youth, including school dropouts, ex-combatants and ex-prisoners." The local area was expected to take these issues into account, along with identified provincial issues, in its planning. Developing decent housing, "human settlement" is the official term, was also a priority. Hmm. Sounded to me like the issues were similar to those in the U.S., though many were no doubt worse in rural South Africa.

Regarding health, the government plan stated: "Primary health care remains one of our focused areas…We managed with the assistance of various stakeholders…to develop five clinics and twenty-two mobile clinics," but more are needed, it said. The main clinic had 6,000 visits a month, about 225 per day, according to the information I'd received from Mrs. Zondo, the clinic administrator. Sam, local program manager of an NGO that I interviewed, and who lived down the road from me in Goodhome, made a direct connection between the high HIV rate and unemployment: "Lack of jobs means that people are free to have sex every day and there are many more opportunities to practice unsafe sex, which leads to a higher rate." I was never able to tie down an official unemployment rate, but it was estimated to be 50-89 percent. The HIV rate in adults aged 18-40 approached thirty-five percent. I would not have made a connection between high unemployment and a high HIV rate, but what Sam, manager of the Meals on Wheels program, said made sense.

Some of my own editorializing for the report, which was encouraged, said, "Imbabazane, like many places in South Africa, has a foot in two worlds: many citizens live modestly, in many ways not unlike ancestors from the 18th, 19th and 20th centuries, but also with a keen sense of modern life in the 21st century. A good example: The proportion of households that had a cell phone increased from 14.5 percent in 2001 to 66.4 percent in 2007, yet only twelve households had access to the Internet from their homes." There still are many people who don't have decent access to water or sanitation, or live in areas not served by electricity.

Many of the people I interviewed, including the clinic administrator, said better water delivery systems were a high priority. Most villages had wells with pumps for people to collect water—that's the way I got my water in Goodhome—but other villages had water delivered by tanker trucks, which sometimes didn't show up, leaving people with no water.

I learned early on that I didn't want to waste water and had wanted to analyze my water usage in the village, but couldn't until I came home to the states and bought a new calculator. I went through three in just a few months. Must have been the dust. I'm kind of autistic that way: a fascination with numbers. I recorded the results of my study in my journal and in a post on Facebook in December 2012:

"As I've explained, I have to walk about 300 meters to fill one of my two five-gallon buckets from the well where I must hand-crank a pump handle 135 times to fill it. I've compiled the stats for the eight full months I've been there—April thru November—and extrapolated what use would have been over the course of one year.

"I filled a bucket 92 times—an average of 11.5 buckets per month—or 460 gallons (690 gallons in a year). That's 12,420 cranks of the pump handle in eight months or 18,630 in a year. Ninety-two buckets in eight months, or 138, extrapolated for over the course of a year. This is water I used for drinking, cooking, brushing teeth, bathing, washing dishes, mopping mud from the floor, and washing laundry, by hand. And making a cup of instant coffee every morning, when I had power to heat water. I find it interesting that I used 18 buckets of water the first month, April 2012, but fewer buckets in each succeeding month. Apparently, I really didn't want to waste water since it's so much work to get it. I don't know what the average monthly per-person use of water is in the U.S., but I suspect it's a lot more than 11.5 five-gallon buckets per month (57.5 gallons). I've also figured, from observing others from the village that use the pump, that, over the course of an average day, approximately 15 buckets per hour get filled, which is about 180 buckets per day during 12 hours of light. (Most black South Africans choose not to get water after dark). That's 24,300 cranks of the pump handle per day, or 8,869,500 over the course of a year. Amazing!" Water for brushing teeth and drinking was filtered in an effective contraption supplied by Peace Corps to every volunteer, but for the rest it came straight from the five-gallon bucket.

Another problem was that many people still cooked over a wood stove, even if they had electricity, because they couldn't afford to use power to cook. Wood burning was also the main way people heated their homes. Residents spend a lot of energy getting wood for cooking and warmth, and water for cooking, drinking, cleaning and bathing. There are still thousands of households "without access to potable water"—ten percent of the population—the government report stated. (The report said "portable" water, but I presumed that was a typo). Poor sanitation was another significant problem, as 14.5 percent of households had no toilets at all, let alone a decent disposal system. One Sunday afternoon, on my weekly walk around the village, I photographed two women who had walked several kilometers carrying small trees stripped of branches. I estimated their bundles weighed 50-75 pounds. I posted a picture of them on Facebook and explained that the wood they carried would be needed for all cooking and heating of water for their families for the next week or so. Then they would have to do it again.

Also worthy of mention, I said in my assessment, was an ambitious provincial program called Sukuma Sahke ("working together" in Zulu), that operates at the local level. The program tasked local municipalities—fifty-one in KwaZulu-Natal—with identifying individuals and families in their jurisdictions who need help. They then arranged for that help to be provided, either locally or by referral to provincial or national social programs. Social work, basically. There were 3.5 million KZN residents who lived below the poverty level who could potentially benefit from this program. Helping Nonhlanhla (who was a ward leader in her village for the program) in her duties became one of my projects. We attended monthly meetings in which each ward reported on its activities of the previous month. Some of the stories were heart-breaking: ward volunteers surveying a household and finding children or elders near death, women abused by husbands who needed immediate intervention, families with little food but a couple of potatoes and no income to buy any.

"What I've presented here is just a smattering of the information and statistics I found in my research for writing my assessment," I wrote in my summary, "but offers a realistic view of the norm in many parts of Africa. I look forward to using this information to decide with my program what my projects will be," I concluded.

The municipality's five-year plan was a treasure trove of interesting information. Among the things I learned about my new home that I didn't include in my CNA:

"HIV and AIDS remain stubbornly high despite aggressive programs by various stakeholders involved in the health sector discouraging irresponsible behavior. The most infected are youth and pregnant women." When I told one young local man I met at a family event about what I was doing in his community he told me, "I will never use a condom. It's not natural." I told him I agreed, but that, "It's better than dying of AIDS." He had no response. Not long before I returned I read that the rates of new HIV cases had started to decline in South Africa. I'd like to think Peace Corps can take some of the credit for that.

The plan continued: "Imbabazane as a municipality in South Africa is a reflection of a broader society, with a dichotomy of rich and poor, skilled and unskilled, those who are well and those are sick. It is characterized by vulnerable groups that find themselves on the margins of society: youth, women, the disabled and those affected by extreme poverty. When social and human development is low, the social fabric of the society begins to disintegrate. This manifests itself in high rates of alcoholism, substance abuse and crime directed at women and children."

I also learned that rural South Africa could teach the U.S. a thing or two about dealing with poverty. The proportion of households living in "informal dwellings" has remained the same over several years, the report stated: "We acknowledge that shelter is a constitutional right for every citizen." How ironic that in my home city of Eugene, and in other U.S. cities, homeless people who use "informal dwellings" (tents) are routinely arrested for sleeping because municipal philosophies in the U.S. aren't as enlightened as those of rural South Africa.

I learned that there are only two factories in all of Imbabazane, a shoe factory and a braiding factory, and that there was consensus that more were needed to improve the area's economy and unemployment rate. A seventy-seven-year-old man I met, Obadiah, a life-long resident of the area, except for the years he worked in Johannesburg, had some ideas. I met him walking on the highway one day and he invited me to his home for tea so he could share his thoughts for improving the economy. I included them in my assessment. He believed that the local government should build a soccer stadium, a shopping complex, a boarding school and a zoo. However, he was unable to say where the money to build these projects would come from. He was one of many colorful people I met during my time in South Africa. Another was a local man I suspected was homeless and perhaps mentally ill (as we would define it in the U.S.), who slept somewhere near Masiphile and whom I often ran into during the day. Thabo (TA-bow) would politely panhandle, often asking for only two rand, about nineteen cents, to buy one cigarette from the tuck shop. I suspect he also had friends who supplied him with alcohol, and probably gave him food and/or a place to sleep. Or perhaps he slept in an abandoned rondavel. In my home town that would be called trespassing and he could be arrested. I occasionally broke my rule about not giving rand to panhandlers and gave Thabo two rand for a cigarette.

My needs assessment ended with a list of proposed projects I could potentially initiate. These projects included starting a support/activity group for people with disabilities; a support group for men who were HIV-positive, to be a companion to the already active women's group; develop a website for Masiphile; develop income-generating projects to support the other services, including a recycling project; and GrassRootSoccer and life skills programs at the nearby primary school. My favorite and most ambitious idea was to start a domestic violence intervention group for men, something I had done in my mental health career and for which there was clearly a great need. It was one project I could never get any traction for because I was unable to find a Zulu man who could co-lead such a group with me, a necessity since I could not speak fluent Zulu and would need a local man to interpret and to give credibility to the effort.

A few days after I finished my assessment I decided it would be a good idea to share it with Councilor Mkhize, since his help would be beneficial for several of the potential projects, and I would appreciate his feedback. I printed a copy, wrote a cover note to explain my assessment and headed off to the municipal building near the library to drop it off. Thus began one of the more bizarre experiences I had during my service, a simple task that would have taken five seconds back home, but took forty-five minutes in a Zulu village.

I tried to hand it to the receptionist, asking that she put it in his in-box or mailbox, but she refused to accept it. She asked me to take a seat while she made a phone call, apparently to see if someone would come up and get it. No answer. She said she would try again in a few minutes. After several more minutes and no action I again asked if I could just leave my envelope for the councilor. She again refused to accept it and said, "Come with me."

She led me into the bowels of the building, down a long hall, to the office of Mkhize's assistant. She opened the door without knocking, told me to enter and closed the door without saying a word. In the room, about the size of an average bathroom in an American home, I saw ten people, crowded together, most standing, since there was room for only two chairs and the large desk. Everyone stopped talking and looked at me.

"I'm sorry," I said. "I didn't mean to interrupt your meeting. I didn't know there were people here. I just wanted to leave these papers for Councilor Mkhize. The woman up front wouldn't take them." No one said a word. After a bit I said, "Would that be possible?" No one said anything and all continued to stare at me, not in anger or annoyance; more like wonderment or confusion. After a long, awkward pause, while I considered what I should do next, the young woman who apparently was his assistant stepped forward, haltingly, and asked if I wanted Mkhize's cell phone number.

"No," I said. "I already have his phone number. I just want to leave these papers for him to read at his convenience. It's not urgent." She said nothing and everyone continued to stare at me. "Would that be possible?" I asked. No response. Finally, after another long pause, she said, quietly, "Yes," and accepted the packet, as if it were a snake. "So, you can see that he gets this?" I asked. Silence and another long pause, then, "Yes."

"Ngiyabonga," I said, using the Zulu word for thank you. I left the building, not at all sure he would get the envelope. I said to myself, "Another lesson in Zulu culture...

but what did I learn?" I sent Mkhize a text message so he would know I had left something for him, but I never heard back from him.

A couple months later when I was in Pretoria for a VSN meeting my colleague Linda, from Bend, who served in Limpopo, a hot, dry province in the north, told the story of a two-day training about financial management she led for black women, from various organizations. One woman, in her fifties, did not say a single word the entire day. The next day, after the last session, the woman shyly approached Linda to thank her for her presentation and shared that she had never been in the same room with a white woman. She had been terrified and intimidated the day before and nearly left, thinking, she said, that she was not worthy of being in the same room with a white person. Internalized oppression. I wondered if that was what was at play at the meeting at the Imbabazane City Hall not long before when hardly anyone would talk with me.

There was a rumor—after that bizarre incident with Mkhize's assistant—that political change was afoot at the municipality. The scuttlebutt was that Mkhize's political fortunes might be about to change, but my source knew no details. It's possible the meeting I inadvertently invaded was about that. Later I learned that Mkhize had been stripped of his secondary title of "deputy mayor"—which, I was told, meant that he lost his two body guards. Nothing else big happened by the time I left—except for his home invasion—and I was left to wonder.

16

GrassrootSoccer, Perma-gardening and Life Skills

Midway between the swearing in and Intermediate Service Training (IST) we learned that in August we would be going to a week-long training event in Empangeni, KZN, a good-sized city in the northeastern part of the province, near the Indian Ocean. Stephanie from Utah and Dan from Chicago were posted there and promised to play hosts when it came time to enjoy the nightlife. (The week was marred somewhat when, toward the end, obnoxious alcohol-fueled behavior by one of us made us all look bad).

This would be different than any other training because it was to include counterparts from our organizations whom we had been working with for several months. Training with counterparts was important because the primary tenet of Peace Corps philosophy is that projects should be "sustainable," the Holy Grail of our development work. These counterparts would continue the work after the volunteer left. For that to be effective, counterparts needed to believe they were as important, perhaps even more so, than the Peace Corps volunteers assigned to their organizations. An equally important concept is "capacity building"—something that happens when a new program is started that didn't exist before—another hallmark of Peace Corps thinking. Three distinct workshops were planned.

We would be staying at a modern conference center with great buffet meals, nice rooms, and nearby evening entertainment. The first few days were devoted to Life Skills training, a program that partners Peace Corps volunteers with locals to teach village learners, aged about twelve to seventeen, important skills. The other workshops were perma-gardening and GrassrootSoccer, easily the most fun, though all were enjoyable and informative.

Most Peace Corps volunteers brought one counterpart to participate in all three of the workshops—a day or two of life skills, three days of perma-gardening, and couple of days of GrassrootSoccer. But there were no hard and fast rules and some of us, me included, brought more than one counterpart. I had planned to bring three—one for each of the segments—but in the end there were two from Masiphile—Welile and Thando. Mlamuli was supposed to be there for the gardening training, but he bailed at the last minute—without telling either me or Nonhlanhla. Welile took his place, staying an extra three days beyond the Life Skills training. When we got back she and I were motivated to plant an additional fifteen beds of vegetables in our garden. That workshop was definitely a success.

According to the Peace Corps Life Skills Manual, Life Skills is "a comprehensive behavior change approach that concentrates on the development of the skills needed for life, such as communication, decision-making, thinking, managing emotions, assertiveness, self-esteem building, resisting peer pressure and relationship skills. Additionally, it addresses the important skills of empowering girls and guiding boys toward new values.

"The program moves beyond providing information. It addresses development of the whole individual, so that a person will have the skills to make use of all types of information, whether it is related to HIV/AIDS, other sexually-transmitted infections, reproductive health, safe mother-hood, or other health issues and other communication and decision-making situations. The Life Skills approach is completely interactive, using role plays, games, puzzles, group discussions and other innovative teaching techniques to keep the participant involved in the sessions." Our goal was to give young people the skills they needed to resist engaging in behaviors that would endanger their health.

An example of how this program uses behavior change principles, according to the U.S. National Academy of Sciences:

"Fear messages have limited use in motivating behavior change. If fear is overwhelming it can hinder, rather than help, efforts to change. Too much fear may cause one to deny they are at risk, to rationalize by pointing to others who have practiced similar behaviors and survived, and to avoid seeking medical care altogether."

The Life Skills program, on the other hand, avoids fear and negativity and instead "focuses on positive messages—creating, maintaining and reinforcing healthy behaviors and working toward a better life for everyone in the community," according to the Peace Corps manual.

Welile and I hoped to identify a school in our community where we could offer this course to a group of co-ed teens. It had been successful in other places and we hoped it would work in our community, too.

Unfortunately for me, Welile got a paying job. She moved on before we could start our life skills program at the school next door, whose principal had given us a green light. I decided I would find another counterpart, perhaps a motivated and outgoing senior from the nearest secondary school, to partner with me. But I was sent home before I could pursue that goal.

My first day in Empangeni I met Sindisiwe (sin-di-SEE-way) —"saved" in Zulu—a Zulu woman who was the counterpart of my colleague Paige from Eastern Washington. Paige's site was an NGO in Nquthu, where Donovan also served. Sindisiwe lived in the nearby village of Island-lwana, an area with many historical attractions, including battlefields made famous by wars between Zulus and the English, and between Zulus and early Afrikaners. Though Sindisiwe looked young, I learned she was twenty-seven, a single mother of boys aged one and five, and spoke English better than most. She had taken language training when she worked at a museum that catered to English-speaking tourists. She was petite with skin the color of dark chocolate. Her main pair of shoes, as with many Zulu women, were a pair of black high heels which she wore most of the time. They seemed cumbersome and dangerous to me, but Zulu women love them, even when walking in dirt or mud. Many Zulu women wear them while walking in mud and never get them dirty. She often wore sweaters over ankle-length dresses.

As the week progressed and I got to know Sindisiwe more—talking at tea breaks, sitting with her at dinner, running into her in the lobby—I came to see that, in addition to being attractive, she was intelligent, funny, principled and dedicated to providing for her family. And her English was about a thousand times better than my Zulu. She lived in a household that had four generations: her two boys (whose father was only minimally in their lives and who lived far away), her two younger brothers, her mother and grandmother. She saw herself as the primary breadwinner for her family, but, common in an area with a seventy-five percent unemployment rate, she had been unable to find steady work despite her clear talent and skills. And she had no relatives who could favor her over others, a practice common in Zulu culture.

Meantime, she volunteered. Her family survived on her grandmother's social security pension, the animals they raised, and the fruits and vegetables they grew in their garden. She did most of the gardening, cooking, cleaning, laundry and caring for the animals. Common in Zulu culture, she was a Jill of all trades. Her circumstances reminded me of one of my favorite Nelson Mandela quotes: "Poverty is not an accident. Like slavery and apartheid, it is manmade and can be removed by the actions of human beings."

A few months after writing the above paragraph I read *Living Poor*, by Moritz Thomsen, a Peace Corps volunteer in Ecuador in the mid- to late 1960s, not long after Peace Corps started. He had been a farmer in Northern California for many years and joined Peace Corps when he was about fifty, and his farm had failed due to economic factors that affected agriculture. He trained in Montana, and was sent to a remote village in Western Ecuador to teach poor villagers modern farming techniques. He served four years in Peace Corps. He wrote:

"When they walk on the beach they are always carrying something—a child slung on the back or hanging from one hip, a basket full of clothes balanced on the head, or baskets of food. They walk with disdain, like royalty condemned to servitude. I don't know of anyone in the rest of the world— with the possible exception of Audrey Hepburn—who in bare feet and rags, loaded down like a pack animal, could give an impression so regal and dignified.

"The women are the serious ones; their job is to hold together the family unit, society itself. They do it with their character and by sheer force of will. The society is matriarchal by default, and secretly. No man would ever admit it, and the women are too wise. They have no protection under the law, for ninety percent of the marriages are common law, but the women, with a fierce but hidden dedication which must spring from a feeling for order and from the maternal impulse to protect their children, somehow keep the society from falling apart.

"This is all women's work: to cook, clean the house and haul water; to wash clothes and care for the children; to feed the chickens, to plant, hoe and harvest the family garden; to pull weeds in the yard, to find oysters and lobsters in the low-tide waters, and to dig clams on the beach; to make clothes for the family, to sew pants and shirts, and then to patch and patch and patch.

"And this is women's work: to stand before God at church on Sunday, representing the family, and to beg for mercy."

I read this, then read it again. And again. It describes well the roles of Sindisiwe and the other black women in rural South Africa—probably in most developing countries. I could not write a better description. After his four years in Peace Corps, Thomsen returned to Sacramento to care for his dying father, and one week after his father died he returned to rural Ecuador to spend the rest of his life farming with Ecuadorian friends he'd made during his service. He died there of cholera in 1991 at the age of seventy-six. He also wrote *The Farm on the River of Emeralds*, a book about his post-Peace Corps life.

I was even more impressed with Sindisiwe when I learned she had left an abusive relationship with the father of her boys, Siyabonga—the five-year-old—and Alondwe, the baby. Domestic violence and emotional abuse are common, and commonly accepted, in Zulu culture. It could not have been easy for her to leave the relationship.

The middle three days of the week were devoted to perma-gardening, a program to teach Peace Corps volunteers and their counterparts how to start and maintain more or less permanent gardens. I've been a gardener to some degree my whole life, having learned much from my father. He grew up in a family of eight kids in Eastern Montana during the Depression, in a family that grew most of its own food. In Peace Corps I learned principles and skills not even my dad, God bless his soul, taught me. We learned about preparing the garden bed, soil management, mulching, building a compost pile, using "kraal manure" (kraal is the Afrikaner word for corral), and inorganic fertilizers, crop rotation, pest and weed management, using pesticides, when to start a seed bed versus buying seedlings, and raising worms to assist in composting. Crop rotation is a principle that helps a garden be "permanent." Different crops use different nutrients in the soil and by rotating crops each season, one crop doesn't deplete the nutrients in one area because next time that crop will be in a different section of the garden. Different crops also add different elements into the soil, which can replenish something depleted by a previous crop.

Perma-gardening was taught by Malapane (mall-a-PAWN-nay), who's main Peace Corps South Africa job was to work in an office and push paper. But, several times a year, when he was able to get away from the office and teach new volunteers about gardening, he was in his element. He loved the outdoor work, shoving his hands into the soil, discussing the merits of kraal manure versus other kinds of manure, answering endless questions he'd probably answered a thousand times before. He praised the small practice plots we planted at a nearby NGO and encouraged us to be creative in our gardens back in our villages. He was one of the more memorable Peace Corps staff I came to know and admire.

Welile's excitement about developing new gardening techniques made the three days we spent learning and practicing them enjoyable and fun. It was also one of the projects that I could count as a success. We already had a big garden, thanks to Mlamuli, but the added produce that resulted from our efforts led us to help even more people in the Imbabazane community, especially those who had chronic illnesses like HIV and TB.

Welile returned to our village after the first two workshops, to be replaced by Thando, who joined me in learning about GrassrootSoccer. GrassrootSoccer was started in 2002 by American professional soccer players who had played in Zimbabwe. When they returned to Zimbabwe to visit, they learned that many of their African friends and soccer players had become ill with HIV or had died of AIDS.

GRS is "an HIV prevention organization that uses the power of soccer to educate, inspire and mobilize communities to stop the spread of HIV and AIDS. GRS trains soccer stars, coaches, teachers and peer educators to deliver an interactive HIV prevention and life skills curriculum to youth aged twelve to nineteen, providing them with the knowledge, skills and support needed to help live healthy lives," according to the GRS handbook. GRS and its partners have provided comprehensive HIV prevention and life skills education to more than 500,000 youth in nineteen countries (South American, European, Asian and Caribbean nations, as well as Africa). Its goal was to reach one million youth by 2014.

One of GRS's partner organizations is now Peace Corps, whose volunteers will help spread the teaching into the rural villages where most volunteers work. Peace Corps Skillz is described by GRS and Peace Corps as "a culture, mindset and toolkit for educators to use when teaching young people about HIV and AIDS." The program creates simple and powerful connections between soccer and life. This approach helps young people have meaningful and relevant discussions about life, take small steps to achieve their goals, stay strong when faced with challenges, and protect themselves and others from HIV. One of GRS's international managers—and one of our instructors in Empangeni—was Kristen Kennedy, Peace Corps volunteer in Zambia before going to work for GrassrootSoccer.

Nombulelo, a South African counterpart to a Peace Corps volunteer, interviewed in the Peace Corps Skillz newsletter, had this to say:

"This program is in high demand because it gives kids so much knowledge without boring them. It makes them excited, and we can tell because they cheer when we come and do not like it when we leave. Due to the increasing rate of dying people, orphans, and hunger or poverty, I feel that it is important to spread the word to this generation about HIV and the dangers of having older sexual partners. Some children get into bad things because of their vulnerability and end up getting infected with HIV/AIDS.

"So, it is my duty to spread this word to warn them about these dangers using GrassrootSoccer. In our culture, it is a taboo to speak about sexual organs. We encourage our GRS participants to use proper names for parts. Although they were surprised and a bit scared the first time we called the organs by their actual Zulu names, as the session continued they felt free to talk openly and asked lots of questions. This was very important because sometimes when kids are assaulted, the criminal goes free because the kids do not know the exact words of the sexual parts, or feel uncomfortable using them. It is our duty to make them feel comfortable talking about their anatomies."

Peace Corps Skillz uses soccer language, metaphors

and activities to address key behaviors that drive the spread of HIV, such as unprotected sex, multiple sexual partners, older sexual partners, and gender-based violence. A typical course has eleven one-hour sessions, weekly, or twice a week, depending on local preference. It was my experience, and I think the experiences of many volunteers, that young people were more receptive to our information, unlike adults, who could be set in their ways, or in denial. It helped that soccer is one of the most popular team sports in the world. Every boy in Africa, and maybe a few girls, wants to be a soccer star.

Thando may have been petite, but she had energy to spare when it came to singing, dancing and game playing. Her kids and the children in our crèche adored her and I was looking forward to partnering with such an exuberant trainer. In our two days of intensive training (shortened from the usual five because we had other things to cover), we learned about "energizers"—a group game or song to get kids excited about starting "practice" and "taking a stand"— controversial statements to get players thinking and debating. These are followed by the thirty-minute lesson of the day, which is interactive and usually resembles a real soccer exercise. During the training, one of the coaches would tell a personal story from a real life experience that touched on the theme of the day. I could tell the story of how two of my high school classmates in the U.S. had died of AIDS. The end of the session involves "cool down," where small co-ed teams debate whether two or three statements about HIV/AIDS are "fact or fiction." And throughout the hour someone would call out a "kilo," a quick shout or cheer, accompanied by a clap, to recognize someone's achievement or good move.

Thando and I planned to present our program to Sakhile School next door to Masiphile and hoped to get in a couple of sessions before an upcoming school holiday break started. But for reasons I never really understood, Thando got cold feet and didn't want to partner with me after all. It's possible she was pregnant. I figured I would corral a "youth ambassador," or student leader, from one of the high schools—perhaps with the help of Councilor Mkhize, and start the program when I returned from Intermediate Service Training. That plan was short-circuited when my mid-service medical exam revealed Parkinson's and I had to return to the U.S.

The week in Empangeni was productive and enjoyable, but perhaps the best part was making the acquaintance of Sindisiwe. Yet, I knew that once we parted company in Empangeni I would never see her again...

17

Sindisiwe, a Zulu Woman

…but I was wrong.

There was much activity afoot Sunday morning, the last day of our week-long training, as several dozen people prepared to return to their villages, an all-day prospect for most of us, who would need to take two or more taxis to get home. I was in the conference center lobby about 7:30, after breakfast, when I saw Sindisiwe, carrying her small bag and wearing her high heels. She was leaving for the taxi rank a quarter mile away to catch her ride back to Isandl-wana. We wished one another well, I told her I was happy to have made her acquaintance, and we parted company. I watched her walk down the circular drive until she disap-peared around the corner of the building.

The taxi I needed would not likely leave before ten, and two hours later I headed for the rank. I quickly found the kombi I needed, made myself comfortable with a book, and waited for the taxi to fill, always necessary before the driver would hit the road. Sometimes this could take several hours. After about thirty minutes I decided I would make a pit stop at the nearest toilet before we left. I got out of the taxi and was looking for the latrine when I saw Sindisiwe sitting in her taxi, also waiting for it to fill. I waved and stopped to offer another good-bye. For reasons that now elude me, I asked Sindisiwe when her birthday was. January 21. I told her I needed to get back to my taxi, but that I would send a text message to Paige on January 21 and wish her happy birthday. She suggested it would be easier to just take her phone number and text or call directly. I thought this was a splendid idea, forgetting the story we had heard from Matt, a more experienced volunteer, who regretted giving his phone number to a local woman. We traded phone numbers as my driver hollered that he was leaving. I said good-bye, again, and, never having made it to the toilet, rushed back to my taxi.

I arrived home several hours later and sent Sindisiwe a text message: "I have arrived home safely. Have you? It was very nice to meet you and spend time with you this week." She answered almost immediately: "Hi & very thank you Gary it was pleasure to me 2 meet u I hope we going 2 meet again, have a goodnight, Oupa" (using my Afrikaner name from Bundu, the word for grandfather).

For the next two months we communicated often via text message and occasionally by phone when cell phone tower reception cooperated. Often, we were thwarted by the frequent spring thunder and lightning storms, or my location in a low-lying area that left me without line-of-sight to the nearest tower. I sent her a couple of letters, not a simple accomplishment. In most rural villages (Isandlwana was no exception), there was no home mail delivery, a service we in the U.S. take for granted. There were post office boxes in Nquthu, but these were not affordable for unemployed rural villagers. This is another reason why cell phone service is so important to black South Africans. During one of our calls Sindisiwe told me she had been kicked in the head that day by a cow. I assessed her over the phone for a concussion, or closed head injury—did she have a headache, or nausea? Were her pupils equal and reactive? I made her promise to go to the village clinic in the morning and get a real assessment. She did and was fine.

The primary school where Sindisiwe attended as a child allowed her, for a time, to have her mail sent there. Eventually, the principal told her she could no longer get her mail there, so I asked a Peace Corps colleague to be a conduit for my letters. But the volunteer declined. It was easier for me to receive letters from Sindisiwe, since I had a post office box in Estcourt that I checked weekly. In her first letter she referred to meeting unexpectedly in the taxi rank in Empangeni: "The time I was in a taxi to my village I wasn't even think to see someone like you Gary. I know it is unusual, as I am a Zulu woman, to communicate with a white guy, because of the language we speak, but I see our communication does not affect each other. We try our best to let someone tell or hear what we are saying." Couldn't have said it better myself. Certainly not in Zulu.

After a couple of months, I suggested we meet in person on a weekend. This would mean each of us would have to take two taxis on a Saturday, an all-day event, to meet in Dundee, a small city not far from Ladysmith, roughly midway between her village and mine. We did this several times over the next few months, spending as much time as we could together. People stared at us, not because she was half my age, which was not unusual in Zulu culture, but because one of us was white and the other black. I was used to being stared at, being the only white face in a sea of 60,000 blacks back in the collection of villages I traveled in Imbabazane. We never held hands, although I wanted to. We never talked about it, but I think both of us understood that holding hands might subject us to more than stares. There are racists in every culture and I think we both knew that it might be dangerous to challenge the norm in more public ways than just walking down the street together. When we would part company on Sunday afternoons I would squeeze her hand, discreetly, for an instant. That had to pass for holding hands. When we arrived in Dundee I often greeted her by saying, "Sobabili"—"the two of us" (and the name of Nonhlanhla's village), and she would respond by smiling and saying, "Simunye,"—"We are together" in Zulu.

Peace Corps, rightfully, frowns on volunteers developing relationships with "host country nationals" in the volunteer's village. If it doesn't work out there could be fallout that affects how the volunteer and, by extension, Peace Corps and America is viewed. There are few secrets in a small village. If I was discreet, being friends with a HCN who lived 150 miles away was probably manageable. I was, and have been, so discreet that to this day only my daughter's family and a few of my closest friends know about Sindisiwe. Most of my volunteer colleagues probably won't know about her until they read this book. Its possible Paige suspected, but I doubt anyone else did.

Sindisiwe told me about her background and family during the time we spent together. I never called her Sindi, as others did, because I thought Sindisiwe was such a pretty name. She had lived in the area her entire life. She grew up in a house with no electricity, no running water, no indoor plumbing. Her family had never owned a television or a car. After dark, candles and lanterns provided light. She had never been to a big city, an airport, a movie theatre, a national park; had never driven a car, nor been in an airplane. On one of our trips to Dundee I learned she had never eaten pizza, so we walked to the nearest pizza joint and ordered one. She liked it. She didn't drink alcohol, and was probably nervous that I had a beer or glass of wine. But, to her credit, she didn't show it. Or maybe she trusted me. Many South

African men use alcohol to excess and it would be understandable for any woman to worry.

There are those who would say I was blind, that she took advantage of me, but I don't believe that. It's true that I spent many a rand on her—airtime vouchers so we could talk on the phone, costs associated with our trips to Dundee, a pair of shoes—not high heels—gifts for her boys, a shirt, a cell phone to replace her broken one, money to buy things her family needed. It is common in Zulu culture for men spend money on their female partners. At times I was frustrated by her belief that I was rich, but, by her standards, I was wealthy. One could even argue that, given that she was the breadwinner for four generations it would have been irresponsible for her to not "use" her new friend to help her family. I choose to believe that her feelings and affection were sincere.

On one of our weekends I decided we would go to the Amphitheater Backpacker north of Bergville for a change, rather than to Dundee. This meant three taxi rides for her instead of the usual two. It was dark before she finally arrived in Bergville and we rushed to get the remaining two seats on the last taxi heading north out of town. There were perhaps twenty people in the taxi designed for fifteen and we were crammed in like sardines. As usual, I was the only white person aboard. We were only a couple of kilometers out of town when Sindisiwe leaned over and whispered that we were the talk of the taxi, all wondering what an *umlungu* was doing in the kombi. I'd had a similar experience a few months earlier when I found myself next to a twenty-five-year-old school teacher who was coming home to his village, Shayamoya ("good air" in Zulu), near mine, on a school break. He spoke English well and told me the taxi was abuzz with chatter about where the white man was going and why.

When I was forced to leave South Africa suddenly, there was no opportunity to see Sindisiwe and properly say good-bye. I had to explain by phone, just a few hours before my flight, that I was leaving, and why. My forced sudden departure seemed hypocritical to me, given Peace Corps philosophy about building relationships in your village. But I wasn't given a choice. In addition to not having a proper good-bye with Sindisiwe, I was unable to say good-bye to most of my friends, and Zungu's family, in Imbabazane.

Early in our relationship Sindisiwe and I had a conversation in which she said she didn't see herself ever leaving her family and moving to the United States. I said I would not want to leave my family either and move to South Africa. There was an expectation on both our parts that our relationship would continue until March of 2014 when I was scheduled to "COS" (close of service) with my SA25 colleagues.

We talked by phone periodically once I was back in the U.S. and planned for her to visit me in Oregon so we could properly say good-bye and give our relationship some closure. I would have to pay her way, but I thought it was important and I wanted to do it. She would need a passport and a visa to visit before we could book her airline reservations. So those were our first goals. I told her how to get a passport from the Office of Home Affairs in her area, and wired her the funds, about $80. It took three months, but she got her passport! Then we began the long, complicated and difficult process of getting a visa—specific permission of the U.S. government to visit for a specific period of time for a stated purpose—a process I described to friends as "a thousand times more complicated" than getting a passport.

The U.S. State Department requires that visa applications be filled out online, and one page printed and brought to the required face to face interview at the consular office in Durban (bay or lagoon in Zulu), rather than the embassy in Pretoria. She wanted to go to Pretoria because it was closer to her home and her cousin who lived there would let her stay at her place. In this case, the steps were required of an unsophisticated Zulu woman from a village with no electricity, let alone a computer and printer and access to the Internet. It would also mean all-day rides, in several taxis, to get to Durban; overnight accommodations—perhaps even two nights—meals, local taxi fares, and finding the consular office in a city of 3.5 million she'd never been to before. I'd been lost in Durban several times.

The logistics were challenging and the barriers perhaps insurmountable. But she was willing to try. There was little I could do to help from my end, other than to wire the funds. All this so she could apply for a visa that might be denied by a U.S. government bent on keeping unemployed people from coming to our shores. Would they really believe that a poor, unsophisticated woman from a remote Zulu village was coming to the U.S. only for a few weeks of "vacation" so she could say good-bye to a Peace Corps volunteer? I thought the chances were less than fifty-fifty.

Fellow volunteers, Kristen from Albuquerque, NM; Donovan from Los Angeles; Cindy from Ohio; and Andrea from New Jersey, during training in Bundu, Mpumalanga.

Me with a baby lion at a wild animal park near Pretoria that some of us visited on the 4th of July, 2012.

Ntabamhlophe, "White Mountain" in the language of the Zulu people. The village where I lived, Goodhome, and several other villages, are at the base of the mountain.

A mud hut in Goodhome, which may have been someone's bedroom, or used for livestock. Attached to a house, a hut like this might be used as a kitchen. Such kitchens are poorly ventilated, contributing to respiratory problems, especially in women and children.

Bhekabantu ("looking after the people" in Zulu), one of my neighbors, shows how we all got our water. It took 135 turns of the handle for me to fill a five-gallon bucket (40 pounds), followed by a 300-meter walk home.

Phila, one of the crèche teachers, encourages kids as they practice their Zulu dance moves.

Kids from the crèche, or preschool, for children aged 1-5. Zulus, especially young ones, love to have their pictures taken, often running up to you shouting, "Shoot me, shoot me!"

Welile (wel-LEE-lay), one of the volunteers I worked with, holds Nonhlanhla's youngest grandchild, Asevala ("continuing" in Zulu), in the traditional Zulu way, strapped to her back. Welile, single mother of an 11-year-old, was Masiphile's most devoted volunteer.

I met these two women, carrying 75-pound bundles of small, cut trees, on a Sunday afternoon walk around the village. They had walked about three kilometers (nearly two miles, each way) to harvest this wood, to be used for cooking food and heating water for bathing and laundry. This amount might last a few days.

One of my Goodhome neighbors putting a traditional grass roof on his new cinderblock rondavel.

Free condom dispenser in the village tuck shop, a common sight in rural South Africa.

Me, with friends, drinking traditional Zulu beer, umqombothi, at the home of Nonhlanhla, Masiphile's program director. It was an event to honor her ancestors, and her sister, Hlengiwe, was also there with her children.

Male and female dancers, both about 15, at a high school Zulu dance competition. I estimated there were at least 2,000 people there. Welile, Phila and I played hooky from Masiphile that afternoon to attend. In Zulu culture breasts are tools for feeding babies and storing cell phones, and it's not considered inappropriate for a teen girl to be topless while performing a traditional dance.

A woman in downtown Estcourt on a Saturday, skinning a cow head in preparation for sale, perhaps to someone who wants to make soup, or use in an ancient ritual.

Sindisiwe

18

Cultural Encounters of the Strange Kind

A couple of weeks before Nonhlanhla and I were scheduled to leave for Pretoria for a big training event, we learned that only one counterpart could join us, instead of the two we had planned to bring: Thando and Welile. Nonhlanhla decided, without seeking my opinion, that Thando—who is also her daughter and Masiphile's financial manager—would be the one to join us there. I thought Welile was a better choice because she volunteered all day every day, in all Masiphile's programs, and was the most dedicated and hardest working of our many volunteers. It would have been a nice reward for her.

I accepted that Thando would be accompanying us, understanding that it was Zulu custom to favor one's own family member over someone else. But Nonhlanhla failed to inform Welile that she wouldn't be going after all. I found out three days before we were scheduled to leave that Welile had not been told when she came to me and asked what I thought the weather would be like in Pretoria, so she could bring appropriate clothing. She was also nervous about not having clothes that were nice enough, though she always dressed nicely at Masiphile. I didn't say anything but the next day I asked Nonhlanhla if she had told Welile she wasn't going with us to Pretoria. She acknowledged she had not, saying she "forgot," and would do it the next day.

The next day, one day before we were leaving, she texted me to say she wouldn't be in because she had meetings at the municipality, and she asked that I "break the bad news" to Welile. But Welile already knew. Earlier that day she had come to me to ask about her bus tickets. I had two choices: lie or tell the truth. I told her the truth. I thought she would be angry and disappointed, but she was relieved.

I spent more time with Welile than with anyone else at Masiphile in my year there. She was thorough, organized, intelligent, willing to do just about anything, loved kids and old people, and got along with everyone. She lived in the village of Emundleni with her mother and ten-year-old daughter. I never learned about the circumstances of why she wasn't with her daughter's father, nor did she ever speak of him, but being a Zulu woman raising a child alone was not unusual. I met her daughter when I gave a presentation at an event for Child Protection Week. I took a picture of her and her cousin and posted it on Facebook.

Jabulani, a government communications official I came to know, gave me and the pastor who prayed that day a ride home since both lived near my place. He asked me for a copy of my remarks, which made me a little nervous. I didn't ask why he wanted them, I just handed him my copy since I could print another the next day. I figured it would annoy my Peace Corps supervisors in Pretoria to read in a newspaper or government website that a Peace Corps volunteer had given a speech without clearing the content with the brass. On the other hand, how could they possibly object to my saying child abuse is bad and parents should protect their kids, not abuse them? In my speech I referenced the United Nation's Convention on Child Rights, which lists forty-two rights every child should have. Surely I wouldn't get in trouble for quoting the UN. A few days later, on my fifty-seventh birthday, I gave the same speech in Sob-abili, Nonhlanhla's village. After the event we all walked to Nonhlanhla's house for a little party for me, with cake and Coca-Cola, what some would consider the national drink of South Africa, second only to Zulu beer.

Not long before I left for good Welile got a paying job as a profiler, a person who goes door to door as part of Op-eration Sakuma Sahke, to survey residents about their needs. I had helped her with her application and assured her she would be an outstanding candidate for the job.

One afternoon the Masiphile staff was all sitting around the créche after the kids had gone. Nonhlanhla started to talk about a grant proposal we had been working on to get funds from the Nestle plant in Estcourt. She took me to task for not completing the application in time to meet the November 30 deadline. The date was November 1, twenty-nine days away from the deadline. My part of the project was done, except for minor edits and finding some prices on office furniture. Fifteen minutes of work, tops. Except for those edits and prices, my part of the project had been done for two weeks. Nonhlanhla, on the other hand, had not yet done anything on her part of the grant request. She still had to assemble letters of support from the municipal-ity and copies of our charter and most recent annual report, documents I didn't have access to.

Welile came to my defense with an appraisal of the tasks yet to be done and the time left to do them. That night I wrote in my journal: *The most bizarre part of this is that I don't think she was trying to make me look bad, nor was she joking. I think she really believes, unbelievably, that there is a problem with getting this project done quickly, and that it's my fault. Strange.* In the mental health biz, we would call that projection—projecting fears about one's own performance onto someone else. In the end she failed to complete her part and we missed the deadline. But Welile had been on my side. And, as always, life went on. A few months later there was a similar situation involving a different grant application, with a similar outcome. I had had one day to complete a lengthy and complicated form, but my laptop was not compatible with the funder's software and I was unable to figure it out by the end of the day. Nonhlanhla was quite angry. That night I wrote in my journal: *Sometimes black South Africans at NGOs have no idea that the things they ask volunteers to do are completely unreasonable and things that they themselves could never do.* The next day all was fine and we were on good terms again. Internalized oppression?

That afternoon incident faded away that night when I had dinner at Mdu and Amanda's house, which always meant a nice time. We were watching a dating show, "All You Need is Love," on television. It included a segment devoted to gay men dating, with the contestant interviewing three candidates for a date. I told Mdu I was surprised that such a show would be on South African television. He agreed. He had never seen the show before. He said that being gay "isn't natural."

"Not to you and me," I told him. "But to a gay person it's completely natural. They were born that way." He laughed, but had no response. I told him that I had many friends back home who were gay and lesbian—and normal. He looked surprised but didn't say anything. It's not likely that I changed his views about homosexuality that night, but I hoped I had opened a door, even slightly, for diversity and tolerance. Maybe the next time the subject came up in his life, Mdu would remember our conversation.

Two weeks later came an event many had been anticipating for some time: graduation of fifteen of our créche kids, nearly half, who had turned five in the past few months. When the new school year started, after the Christmas holiday, they would be attending the public schools in their respective villages and a new crop of toddlers would replace them. Zulus know how to throw a party, even if they're a little late out the starting gate. Families had been told the event would start at 10 a.m. At 8:45 Nonhlanhla, Busissisiwe, the cook, Thando, Welile and the two créche teachers, Philder and Phila, gathered and began to plan the day. Four of them were to go to town to shop for the food and supplies for the seventy-five or so people (kids, families, staff, and local dignitaries) who had been invited. Each had a list and knew which store to go to for their purchases, with money I suspect was supplied from Nonhlanhla's personal resources, since Masiphile didn't have any funds. Meanwhile, men were erecting a huge canopy—common at many outdoor Zulu functions to protect people from rain or sun, or both—and setting up tables and chairs. We started the event at 1 p.m., though people started arriving at ten. At 12:45, fifteen minutes before we would start, Nonhlanhla told me she wanted me to be the "program director of the day," sort of like a master of ceremonies.

She asked me to type up a program and print out several copies, which I was able to do only because someone back home donated the money to buy Masiphile's first printer. (For a non-techie like me, it was a bitch to set up. The instructions included ten languages, but none was English. I think I got help from Christopher in Bergville, via text and email. It wasn't the first time, or the last, he helped me with technical matters that baffled me. My talented daughter back home, Megan, also helped many times, via email).

I sat at the head table with Nonhlanhla, the guest speaker and others and I literally was two seconds from welcoming everybody, in Zulu, when, low and behold, Welile stood up and started doing the same thing! She went on to assume all the MC duties. I became the official photographer. She did a fine job and the day ended successfully, despite my having been unceremoniously replaced without warning two seconds before we started. Another day learning about Zulu customs. Oh, and at the church next door, about forty meters away from our event, church members were slaughtering a cow for a weekend gathering. I took a picture of the five-year-old crèche graduates receiving their certificates in their caps and gowns in the foreground, while the unlucky bovine's throat was being slit in the background. No one but me seemed to notice.

Our other neighbor was Sakhile Primary School, with which we had a lot of contact. Many of our volunteers' children were enrolled there, and many of our graduating crèche kids would attend Sakhile. I met with the principal, Mr. Knihle, several times. He always wore a nice suit and drove a BMW. On National Public Service Day, July 18 and Nelson Mandela's birthday, learners from the primary school gave our building a thorough cleaning. I took lots of pictures. The idea was that everyone should spend sixty-seven minutes that day volunteering. Sixty-seven was the number of years that Mandela spent in public service pursuing freedom for his people, often, and famously, at his own peril.

All of my interactions with the school seemed tame and routine compared to the one I had a couple of months before I came home for Christmas in 2012.

"There's no such thing as 'separation of church and state' here," I wrote in a blog post at the time. *"Such a concept, the law of the land in the U.S., would absolutely baffle most black*

South Africans," I continued. *"Their religion, Christianity for the most part, is interwoven throughout every aspect of their lives, though they also maintain many Zulu traditions that may be thousands of years old, and some of which might offend Western Christians. Of course, this also means that many other religions are not represented at government functions, while people who practice those religions are forced to participate in Christian practices they may not believe in, if they want to participate in their government. Many people think this is wrong (my mother wouldn't be one of those) which is why, in the U.S., we separate the two. I make no judgments here; am merely reporting my observations."*

Almost every morning at Masiphile we started the day with a spiritual song or two, then someone would pray. Mlamuli, the gardener, usually wasn't there yet, so it was me and six or so women. I couldn't sing along because they sang in Zulu, but I could clap and hum. Occasionally, they would ask me to pray, which I was happy to do, having grown up in a prayerful, church-going Protestant family. My prayers always started in Zulu: "Siyabonga, Baba"—"We thank you, Father"—then continued in English. One day the women asked me if there were spiritual songs from America I could sing for them. The only one I could think of was "Jesus Loves Me," which I'd known since childhood. I sang it for them and they all recognized it and sang it for me in Zulu. Then they asked me to sing "The Star Spangled Banner," so I did. Thankfully, that was the end of my singing that day.

One morning we learned that four or five students at the school next door had told a teacher a few days earlier that they had seen a woman with blood on her arm, but she wasn't a real woman. She was a ghost or an apparition. The teacher apparently told the principal, who I would describe as intelligent, sophisticated and highly educated.

This came to me second hand from co-workers who lived in the nearby village, Shayamoya, so I don't know exactly what transpired next, but after a few more days it was announced there would be a "day of prayer" at the school. As next-door neighbors and partners in various activities, we were expected to be there, so Welile and I marched over to represent Masiphile.

About one hundred people, in addition to the learners, sat under a huge canopy. At the head table were eleven ministers from various churches, dressed in suits, and carrying their bibles, ready to quote scripture if given the opportunity. The head table also included the principal and Mkhize, our local politician. As usual, I was the only white person present. Anytime I got invited to a community event I was always asked to sit at the head table. Sometimes I had to say a few words, but, if I was lucky, I did not. I was always honored to be treated as someone special, but it's not my nature to seek the limelight, so it was something that took some getting used to—especially when I had to speak Zulu.

The festivities had already started when I sat down at the front table. They put me at the end on the left, next to speakers the size of Volkswagens. I recognized a couple of our crèche teachers, parents of some of our kids, and a few women from our elders' group. Several local congregations were represented, each distinguished by the distinctive congregational attire they wear—black and white, or blue, or green and white, what amounts to uniforms—just as learners in all public schools have uniforms in the school colors.

There was a lot of singing, praying, dancing, and pandemonium, common at all Zulu functions, and all of it amplified about forty decibels higher than it needed to be (in my opinion). In my journal that night I wrote that the music was *so loud it made my thighs vibrate, making me think my phone was vibrating. It wasn't."* The soloist was a hefty Zulu woman with a wonderful voice and impressive range, right up there with Diana Ross, Gladys Knight and Whitney Houston, talented gospel singers in the U.S. before they went on to become famous entertainers.

Eventually, someone asked everyone at the head table their names and what they did, or who they represented. I was asked if I was a pastor, even though I was in my sheep herder vest and dusty hiking shoes, not knowing until just a few minutes earlier I would be sitting at the head table in front of hundreds of people. This sort of thing often happened. I would the last to know my part in important events, often just minutes before having to "perform." Gotta be flexible and adaptable, they hammered into us in training. Fortunately, flexibility is in my nature. I didn't look anything like the actual ministers, but I was mistaken for one. I wondered if that was good or bad.

The ceremony went on for two or three hours, culminating in a loud and energetic half-hour message by the main speaker about casting out demons, fighting Satan and cleansing the school of evil. "When the cat's away, the mice will play," the minister said, explaining why it was necessary to bring prayer and gospel to the school to chase the demons (mice) away. He referred to Matthew 8:28-32, a story about Christ dealing with two possessed men. It was akin to an exorcism, I thought. An effort to chase evil from the school. And I mean no disrespect. It's important for Peace Corps volunteers, and anyone learning a new culture, to understand that the people they are living with may have been practicing their beliefs for thousands of years while at the same time trying to integrate in modern ways.

We had to remember that there are practices and beliefs from our Western culture that might seem just as strange to rural South Africans. Though South Africans in many ways embrace modern practices and ideas, one can't expect them to suddenly forget about cultural mores that have been in play for a thousand years. I had never seen anything like this event, though I imagine there are some American churches that have similar practices. Is not exorcism a tenet of Catholicism? And are there not fundamentalist churches in the Southern U.S. who handle venomous snakes as part of their religious services; services where some people have been bitten dozens of times? I assure you my Zulu friends, many of whom are terrified of snakes and consider them evil, would find that quite strange. Zulus often believe and trust traditional healers—what Westerners might call "witch doctors." It's another example of change coming slowly. I remember being pleasantly surprised when I read in one of the Durban newspapers that fifteen traditional healers had completed a two-week course sponsored by the government that certified them to be entry-level HIV counselors. They could then refer people for testing and hand out government-supplied condoms and information. Progress.

Councilor Mkhize spoke last, watched over as always by his two armed body guards. The formal part of the program ended as all school, NGO and government events do, with a final prayer to Baba (father or God) and a song or two and more dancing and clapping. Welile and I left, not realizing that pap with chicken and vegetables were being served. I was sorry later when I heard I missed the meal as my power was out, which meant a peanut butter and jelly sandwich and an apple for dinner.

A few months later I met Amy from SA26, one of our newest VSN members, who told me about "demons" invading her school, a story similar to mine. A student was said to have fainted when she saw blood on her plate at lunch time. Then other learners saw the blood and fainted too. Preachers came, teachers led their classes in singing religious songs, but, the demons remained. Sangomas, traditional healers, were to be brought in to cleanse the school, but I never learned the outcome.

A few weeks later I again found myself in the limelight. Nonhlanhla told me that the next day, instead of coming to Masiphile I should report to the wetland area next to the tar road between Dutch and Sobabili for an event involving several of the village schools and Operation Sukuma Sahke community profilers, about four hundred people altogether. The event, "Safe Sex and Environmental Awareness," called for students and others to clean up the swampy area, with trash to be buried by municipal workers. This would be followed by speakers who would talk about safe sex practices. Nonhlanhla asked me to take a few pictures. Councilor Mkhize was the moderator of the event and introduced me when he saw me in the crowd. I had worn my rattiest pants and tee shirt, figuring I would help with trash, which might include discarded condoms since it was an area where teenagers often went at night to, um, socialize.

I learned the preaching part of the day's events would happen at the Dutch Community Center, not at the wetland, so I tried to sneak away so I wouldn't have to listen to the speakers. But Mkhize saw me and offered me a ride to the center so I couldn't avoid further participation. At the community hall I found an obscure seat in the back, but before long one of the organizers saw me and insisted I sit on the stage up front, in my muddy clothes, in front of 400 people. I protested, to no avail and had to drag my chair with me since there were none left on the stage. In my journal that night I wrote, *"Once again, I looked foolish because Nonhlanhla failed to fill me in on what was really going on and what my role would be.*" At the time, I was annoyed. But now I believe that nobody there noticed or cared that I was dressed in dirty clothes or had mud on my boots and didn't really have a role in the event. I understand that I was being honored. I also understand that its possible Nonhlanhla, who also didn't have a part, was unaware of the second half of the program. In any case, it's a memory I now treasure and I appreciate the cultural forces that were in play.

19

Don't Let Granny Get Hold of You

There were some aspects of Zulu culture that I admired a lot and that could not have been easy at times to practice. Domestic violence is a huge problem in South Africa, though there were few occasions, in my experience, when it was talked about openly, other than in training. But I had a good lesson one day in how the grannies dealt with it.

It was a Wednesday, late morning, the day our gogos met. Dark, angry clouds in the distant western sky were a portent of things to come. Several of the gogos had arrived early and were visiting in plastic chairs lining Masiphile's porch. Just through the gate, next to the cell phone tower that was a prominent landmark, a young man and young woman, twentyish, were engaged in a heated argument. She was attempting to leave and he was trying to stop her by moving in front of her when she tried to walk away. Eventually, the argument escalated into shoving and pushing. We watched the altercation and I wondered at what point intervention should be attempted. When he punched her in the face? When she was screaming for assistance? Should I do it alone? Should I enlist the aid of others? Would they respond or are they so used to such displays that they would do nothing? Would there be any point in calling the police? I favored getting several of us to approach and surround the woman to protect her without openly engaging the young man.

The scene unfolding before us was troublingly reminiscent of an incident I witnessed in my home town a few years earlier along a public bike path next to a high school. A woman was trying to escape from a man who would not let her leave. I watched from about one hundred feet away. When he continued to bully and then grabbed her and held on tight, I called 911 and reported "potentially imminent domestic violence" and described what was happening. The 911 call taker said an officer would be dispatched, but before he arrived the couple stopped quarreling and walked away together. From a distance it seemed voluntary on her part. It's possible he was holding a knife at her ribs that I couldn't see and her leaving with him wasn't at all voluntary. I never knew.

Suddenly, three of the gogos arose as one and started toward the couple, about forty meters away. As the women approached, the pushing and intimidation climbed a notch to hard shoving and the woman swung at the man, just as the gogos arrived and surrounded her. It took less than a minute for the grandmothers to intimidate the young man into letting the young woman go. They talked to him about the error of his ways until the woman was out of sight. Eventually, he took off in the direction of the woman, no doubt planning to pick up where he left off before the gogos intervened. I doubt any one of us had illusions that the gogo intervention solved the problem. It only postponed it until it could resume in a less public place.

The grannies returned to Masiphile and I asked one of them, Celestina, what they had told the young man. She said they focused on talking to the woman, and told her to call police. But the man had taken her cell phone and refused to return it, a common action by abusive men who don't want their women calling for help. I'd seen it before.

Celestina also told me they learned that the man was the father of the young woman's baby, and that the girl's family had told him "he could do whatever he wanted to her" to get her to behave in a manner acceptable to him. I suspect this is disturbingly common. Celestina also said the young woman feared sexual assault as well as physical abuse.

Celestina said his behavior demonstrated "a complete lack of respect" for his elders. I pointed out that he respected, or feared, them long enough to let the girl go. "He strutted around like he was proud of the way he acted," she said. She was disgusted. And surprised and disappointed when I told her that such things also happen in the United States.

I couldn't find specific statistics on the Internet that ranked South Africa against other countries in terms of violence against women, but I'd heard from multiple sources in the time I'd been there that it is among the highest in the world. According to a website called womeninaction.co.za, the South Africa Department of Justice reports that one in four South African women is a survivor of domestic violence; and People Opposing Women Abuse (POWA) states one in six women who die in Gauteng Province, the most populous (Joburg area), are killed by their intimate partners. In 1999 the Institute of Security reported that ninety percent of women interviewed said they had been victims of physical violence, and seventy-one percent of sexual violence. Unarguably, it's a big problem. On Valentine's Day 2013, not long before I left, white South African Olympic runner Oscar Pistorius was arrested for killing his girlfriend. He said it was an accident, that he thought he was shooting a burglar when he fired four shots through a closed bathroom door, hitting her three times. A year later I followed his trial for murder in the press. The same day Pistorius shot his partner, elsewhere in South Africa four other women were killed by their male partners. In some cases children were murdered as well. All on the day of love.

Some of my female Peace Corps colleagues volunteered with domestic violence intervention programs, or at larger NGOs that had such services as a component of their organization. Failure to start a project in my village that helped address domestic violence was one of my biggest disappointments when I headed home.

20

'Village Life is Amazing'

"Village life is amazing," I posted in a blog entry a few months after moving to Goodhome.

It didn't take long for me to get into a routine for the rest of my time in KZN, although it was interrupted periodically by trips to Pretoria or other cities for training or meetings. I would wake up, without an alarm, between 5:30 and 6 a.m., as I had done daily for thirty-five years before I retired. I turned on the radio to catch the news and weather, hit the outhouse, and fixed a breakfast of oatmeal and fruit (no milk since my limited electricity wouldn't support a refrigerator) and instant coffee. If there was no power to operate my two-burner hotplate breakfast was what dinner might have been the night before—a peanut butter and jelly sandwich and an apple, and dried fruit. If power failed I still had music and news because I also had a battery-operated radio.

Occasionally I would fetch water in the early mornings since often there were long lines at the village pump later in the day. That meant a 300-meter walk with a five-gallon bucket, that weighed forty pounds when full of water. Water that would never be wasted, given the energy needed to acquire it. Other villagers at the pump sometimes offered to let me go to the head of the line, which made me uncomfortable. I asked Nonhlanhla if it was because I was white, male, or old. She laughed and assured me it was the latter. Occasionally, a child would offer to pump water for me, or the old gogo who lived next to the pump would tell the children pumping or waiting, to defer to me. Most of the kids were girls, about eight to thirteen, but even a girl as young as eight or nine could balance forty pounds of water on her head, though some used smaller buckets. The young girls laughed, thinking it was funny that I carried my water by the bucket handle. When I could, I would wait my turn and pump my own water. But when the neighbor lady hollered at the kids at the pump and they motioned for me to go ahead, I honored her effort—in "it takes a village" fashion—to reinforce manners and respect for old folks.

When there were twenty or more people waiting for the pump I was reminded of a story told in training about a remote village that, after many years, finally got a government-installed well and pump to replace the women's daily trips to a nearby river to bathe, wash clothes and collect water. But it wasn't long before the new pump was more-or-less abandoned. The women returned to the river because it wasn't just about the water. The river trips were also their way to socialize and get support from friends and neighbors, get caught up on village gossip, and to have others help keep an eye on their children. And they perhaps didn't have cell phones.

On one trip to the well, at night, I met two old men I hadn't seen before. They were using the pump in the dark so I held my flashlight (what South Africans call a torch) so they could see what they were doing. One of them asked me for a few rand, saying he was hungry. I gave him the party line about not having any rand to give away and then, for reasons that now elude me, I added that, "Just because I'm white and American that doesn't mean I have money to give away. I'm a volunteer. That means I work for free." I wasn't nasty about it, I was matter of fact. But I felt bad, that it hadn't been necessary to add that bit about being an American. They were filling two buckets and had let me fill my one first. I said good night to them, hustled back to my place, rounded up my last carrot, a few slices of bread, a package of crackers and an apple and raced back to the pump. But they were gone and I never saw them again. I reminded myself that I needed to remember the lines I wrote in an essay for my hometown newspaper not long after I came to KwaZulu-Natal: "The impression they have of me is the impression they will have of all Americans. That's a big responsibility, one I take seriously. I'm also the first Peace Corps volunteer ever in this collection of villages, so I will set the standard for those who may follow."

The next day, a Sunday when most people were at church, a young man about eighteen introduced himself as Mlengi and said he was a senior in high school. "But you can call me Linge," he said. "That's my hip-hop name." We talked about his desire to go to college and he told me he had seen me around the village but had been afraid to talk to me. I encouraged him to talk to me anytime.

Morning was also when I bathed, in what we called a "bucket bath"—a round, plastic tub about two feet across and ten inches deep, with about three inches of water in the bottom, some of it heated and mixed with cold water, if there was power to use the boiling kettle. I'd stand in the water and wash using a bar of soap and a small pitcher to rinse, carefully so as not to get too much water on the floor. In winter this was no fun—since it might be thirty degrees (F) outside and only cold water available. I usually bathed every other day—daily when it was hot. I washed hair only on the alternate days, or took a sponge bath instead of a bucket bath. Arlene had told us in training that there were periodic cases of Peace Corps volunteers who declined to bathe regularly and that it got so bad at times that their African supervisors would call Peace Corps to complain. I'd toss the used water out the door, sometimes fooling the chickens into thinking I was tossing food scraps their way. Cleanliness is important in Zulu culture, though it's often not always convenient to maintain. I used as little water as possible since I had to carry it a long distance and pump it by hand. I actually had two of those plastic tubs since I also used them for laundry—one for washing by hand and one for rinsing—and for washing dishes.

One day I journaled about hand washing: … *something we think of in the U.S. as simple, quick and known to be effective at preventing the spread of germs and bacteria. How ironic that it's so difficult to do at times, even for Peace Corps volunteers who understand its value. Routinely, I go all day without hand washing, or am able only to rinse in cold water because soap and water, warm or otherwise, are so unavailable. To their credit, the crèche teachers understand the importance of washing and teach the practice to the kids as best they can. And they monitor how the children use the spigot on the rain-filled "Jojo" water tank so none is wasted. Wasting water at times results in punishment, including corporal punishment.*

Mr. Zungu left around six in the morning, sometimes alone, at times with one of his male relatives who drove while he slept, chatted or did paperwork. If I had to get to Masiphile earlier than usual, and we were leaving at the same time, they would give me a ride since they passed by it on the way to Bergville.

Not much later, about 7:20, I left to catch the taxi, a three-minute walk to the main dirt road. Depending on how long I had to wait for a taxi, this would get me to Masiphile between 7:45 and 8 a.m. Sometimes a taxi with room came by almost immediately. Other times they would be running less frequently, or would be full and pass me by. In that case, the driver would signal his taxi was too full to cram in even one more passenger: right hand in a fist, flat left hand tapping on the top of the fist, as one might do to show you were trying to squeeze one more soccer ball into a stuffed gym bag. Sometimes the signal was to flash the headlights to acknowledge you, but indicating he couldn't stop. Sometimes half-full taxis would sail on by because they were full of teachers heading for Edilini School down the road and the taxi was for that purpose, and he wasn't supposed to stop. Sometimes he would point behind him, indicating there was another taxi coming along. In any case, one had always to signal by holding up an index finger to let the driver know you wanted him to stop. A few times, no taxi would come along and I would start walking, taking the short cuts Mdu had shown me. My practice became that if a taxi hadn't come along by the time I was halfway to my destination I would walk the entire distance, about five kilometers (three-and-a-half miles), which took about an hour and a quarter. Good exercise and I saved five rand. Occasionally, an old baba who was one of my neighbors would stop in his old Datsun pickup and offer me a ride. He often also picked up an old woman who had bags and buckets of vegetables she took to the main tar road to sell to passers-by.

When I returned home at the end of the day I would tell the driver where I wanted out by yelling *"isonto!"* (ee-SAWN- toe)—"church" in Zulu. The church, a prominent feature in the neighborhood, was Seventh Day Adventist and was heavily attended each Saturday. It stood at the intersection of the big dirt road and the small dirt road that lead to my home. Many days, however, Dlamini, Thando's husband, would give me a ride home since he had to drive through Goodhome to get to their village about fifteen kilometers further down the road. On the days that he dropped off Welile, Phila and Nonhlanhla—and Thando and their three children were also in the car—we talked and became very close. Often I was in the back seat, wedged between Welile and Phila and holding a child or two in my lap. Being fatalistic rural South Africans, we didn't usually bother with seat belts, which weren't very accessible anyway.

I often counted passengers on the morning commute to pass the time until my stop. Taxis, most of them Toyota vans that resembled old Volkswagen mini-buses, were designed to hold thirteen to sixteen passengers, but often held many more. The record for me was twenty-seven, on a morning when in addition to the usual people heading for the municipal building, the library, or the high school, there were more than the usual number of mothers carrying babies or toddlers to the clinic. Sometimes mothers had more than one child and would plop one child, without asking, into the lap of the nearest passenger. A few times, that was me. The locals understood that on another day they might be the one who needed a little extra help. The cost of a ride: five rand, about forty-five cents, preferably in exact change. Payment was to be made sometime before disembarking. Only once in fourteen months did a driver think I tried to get out without paying. He hollered, only to be corrected by several passengers, who assured him they had seen me pass my fare forward. Drivers were pretty good at keeping track of who had paid and who hadn't, given the large numbers of people entering and leaving over the course of several miles. Sometimes it was left to the honor system to ensure that everyone paid. I must have seen thousands of taxis and only twice did I see female drivers. One was in the village and the man next to me said she was filling in for her sick husband. The other was in Durban.

A typical day at Masiphile for me, if there was such a thing, might begin with checking email. I didn't have access at home because I wasn't close enough to a cell tower. If we had power at Masiphile, which was most of the time, I might make another cup of instant coffee using the electric kettle; we didn't have a stove, and used propane to cook meals for the créche kids. If the power was out at home, as it often was, that might be my first cup of coffee of the day. The teachers were usually already there by the time I arrived. Parents dropped off their children around 7:15. Many of the kids arrived via what amounted to a village carpool, with one parent dropping eight or ten kids at once. Those whose fathers were taxi drivers dropped them before heading off on their routes. We had 35-40 kids enrolled in the créche. There were a few days in winter when there was snow or ice, or it was much colder than usual, and only three or four kids would arrive. I can remember only one day when no one showed up. The teachers went home. There was no system to notify families of a snow or ice closure day at school.

Sometimes we had no power because of a power outage somewhere along the lines that led to our villages. But most of the time we lost power because Nonhlanhla hadn't kept track of the meter and we just ran out. When that happened, someone would have to walk a kilometer to the car wash to buy a voucher with a PIN so we could get back to business. When no one had any money we'd spend the rest of the day doing things that didn't require power.

Masiphile had no well nearby. Instead we had a "Jojo," the brand name for a large, green, round heavy-duty plastic water tank with a brass spigot that sat atop a concrete base, and collected rain water from drainpipes connected to the metal roof. It held 5,000 liters—about 1,250 gallons—and was used for everything: cooking, cleaning, drinking, hand washing, rinsing out dirty diapers, washing dishes. It never ran dry, though it may have come close in summer. The water wasn't filtered and though it was clean when it hit the metal roof, before it got into the tank it had washed dust and bird crap into the gutters, which then drained into the tank. It also had a three-inch diameter hole at the top that permitted insects and who knows what else to enter the tank. I wondered what the purpose of that hole was until we had a whopper of a rainstorm—a deluge, including marble-sized hail stones, non-stop for thirty or forty minutes. It rains a lot in western Oregon, but rarely like it did that day. The tank quickly filled and excess water began to pour out the hole—a gallon or two per second, I would guess. Without that overflow hole the tank could have burst and damaged the building—or worse.

Welile usually arrived before I did, which was good, because I didn't have a key. Separate keys opened the left half of the building where the crèche was located, and the right side where the rest of us worked. Days when I got there first I would hang out with the kids until Welile arrived to let us in. On those days when Welile wasn't coming in, or Nonhlanhla had a meeting and Thando didn't come in until noon, I hung out with the kids and the teachers for several hours. I asked once why we couldn't just get another key, but there didn't seem to be an answer. "Oh, well," I thought, "TIA." Not that I minded helping out with the kids. Those were some of my most enjoyable times. I had many opportunities to practice saying, "Sanibonani, abantwana,"—"Good morning, children," and the children frequently said "Sawubona, ubabamkhulu," or "Good morning, grandfather!" to me.

No two days were exactly the same and in the course of a "typical" day I might interact with the children—often taking pictures of them, work in the garden, walk to the tuck shop for a loaf of bread, about nine rand or eighty cents, or "biscuits" (what Americans would call cookies), research funding opportunities on the Internet and write grant proposals, or accompany Nonhlanhla to a meeting. Researching and writing funding proposals was something I tried to teach to Welile, to make the skill sustainable.

Many days I worked on specific projects like the marketing program to help the gogos sell their handmade products in the U.S., or on the sign project I cooked up to direct drivers to our location, a hundred meters down a dirt road from the highway. The sign, designed by me, also listed all our programs and provided our address and phone number. And was paid for, $222, by what I told people at the time was an "anonymous donor" from the U.S. I was the anonymous donor, because, like most of the older volunteers, I had resources back home, unlike the twenty-somethings. I had a modest pension that I could fall back on when necessary, easily accessible from the bank in Estcourt with a debit card. (The generosity of sixty-one-year-old Greg from Seattle, a retired contractor, could fill an entire book with stories about projects he personally funded in his village). It took several months from the time when I had the idea for the sign to the day it was installed. Thanks to logistical issues, when the sign was finished at the sign shop in Estcourt, it was too big to fit in a taxi. When Mkhize tried to bring it in his bakkie, it wouldn't fit in there either. Finally one day we were all going to an HIV/AIDS meeting in Ladysmith, in a government van. On the way back, late in the afternoon, I asked the driver if he could stop at the sign shop, only a few blocks out of the way. We got there just before closing time and were able, just barely, to wedge the sign in through the sliding side door. Mission accomplished!

I also spent a lot of time working on the website I built for Masiphile. My talented graphic designer daughter, Megan, did the creative artwork, my website-building friend Tim Mueller of GreyWolf Projects (gwproj.com) did the behind-the-scenes technical work, and I took the photos and wrote the copy. Megan and Tim donated many hours of talented work to help me complete this project. The website is masiphile.org. Feel free to visit it and make a donation.

A couple of times a week I would walk to the library to turn in a book or two and visit with Mdu and the other librarians. At least weekly there would be a meeting at the library or the municipal building, usually with Nonhlanhla, but sometimes I alone would represent Masiphile. Lunch came with the territory most days, usually pap served with gravy and vegetables, prepared by Busisisiwe and brought to us after the children had been served. One day she was running a little late and asked me if I was hungry. "I'm a man," I told her. "I'm always hungry...But no hurry," I said. "Good food is like good sex. The longer you wait, the better it is." Fortunately, no one was offended and all laughed.

On one of my walks to the library I encountered three young men, twentyish, who stopped me to talk. I'm sure they had seen me around and wondered about the white man in the village. I explained that I was a volunteer at Masiphile where, among other things, we try to help people who were HIV-positive and, through education, to prevent further infections in the villages. One of the young men, Khanyile (con-YEE-lay), who was intoxicated, told me he was HIV-positive and was depressed about it. He said that was why he was drunk so much of the time. Both his friends said they were worried about him, especially about his drinking.

Back home in the U.S., working in a public mental health program, this was the point where I would have explained that "alcohol is a central nervous system depressant, the ingestion of which will, in addition to the circumstances, contribute to further depression"—or something like that. But that didn't seem like the proper response there on the tar road in the middle of Sobabili in HIV/AIDS-ravaged rural South Africa. I asked him if he was in treatment at the Ntabamhlophe Clinic, where he could get anti-retroviral medication, the best treatment for HIV. He said he wasn't. He implied he was just waiting to die. I encouraged him to go to the clinic and get into treatment, to reduce his drinking and eat healthy food. I told him my name and encouraged him to stop by anytime—that I was usually there most days—if he wanted to talk more. We parted company and I never saw him again. I've always regretted that I didn't get his phone number or give him mine, so that I could follow up and support him. Occasionally, I fantasize that he did go to the clinic, get into treatment, improve, get a handle on his drinking and stop to thank me for helping him. But that was a fantasy. Then I think about Miss Lillian and the story about how volunteers may never know of the impacts they made. The probable reality is that Khanyile continued on his downward path and may be dead now, just months after I left the village…but maybe his friends were listening.

Many days Welile or Nonhlanhla would turn on religious music they had programmed into Nonhlanhla's huge, fifteen-year-old Dell computer and play it—much louder than I liked—while we worked. Some days it was a recording of a sermon, by a preacher who yelled as if possessed, about the evils of this or that and the importance of following God. The same sermons I'd heard back home, but these were in Zulu and louder! I must have heard that sermon a hundred times. But most days it was a low-key, relaxing atmosphere and through it all there was much conversation and many opportunities to educate one another about our respective cultures. Some days more cultural education and gossip ensued, than actual work. Then there was the day Nonhlanhla was called to the hospital in Ladysmith for a family medical emergency when a bureaucrat from the provincial Department of Social Development was supposed to come by to pick up a quarterly report that was overdue. Nonhlanhla called and ordered us to lock the doors, turn out the lights, draw the blinds and be very quiet. "Pretend that no one's there so he will just go away." Ironically, he never showed. And I missed another playing of the loud sermon.

I've always been fascinated by snakes and Africa has some of the most potentially deadly ones in the world. I wouldn't want one for a pet, and I don't like to touch them, but I understand their importance in the ecosystem—eating rodents and insects and all—and I'd never kill one if I could avoid it. I once helped a fourteen-year-old autistic boy transition from an orphanage in Oregon to a foster home. He had a corn snake about four feet long—a common non-venomous pet and usually docile. The boy insisted I let it crawl up my arm. He was testing me and I wanted to connect with him so that he would trust me, so I held my breath, looked the other way, and let the snake slowly make its way up my arm. Intellectually I knew it was harmless, but I hit the pause button when the snake started to encircle my neck. I asked the boy to remove his friend. He laughed and so did I. The placement was a success.

I liked to ask people if they had ever seen black mambas or cobras or other venomous snakes. Nonhlanhla said she never had, though she had lived in the area her entire life. It didn't seem likely. I wondered if she really had seen some of those snakes but had blacked out a memory that would have been quite frightening. Same with Welile, who also told me that venomous snakes can tell the difference between black people and white people and prefer to bite blacks. I laughed, believing that she was joking. It soon became clear she was not. A few weeks later I posed the question to Sindisiwe, expecting her to laugh at the absurdity of the concept, but, instead, she agreed it was true. Internalized oppression or silly "old wives' tale"? One Friday I told Welile I was going exploring over the weekend and for the first time planned to walk across the new pedestrian bridge that spanned a large swampy area in a small valley between Goodhome and Sobabili. It had been there only a year or so, and cut several kilometers off the walk between the two villages. She was aghast at the thought and said that she would never walk across that bridge because if she did she would be attacked by huge venomous snakes. I crossed the bridge several times and never saw a snake, only the pretty wildflowers and the occasional heron.

I did see a few snakes that had been killed by cars, but only once did I see a live snake, in Africa, in Giants Castle, the provincial park near Goodhome I visited a couple of times. It was gray and white and about a foot long, probably non-venomous. I saw it only for a second on a hiking trail in tall grass. Most snakes in South Africa are non-venomous, but it's the potentially dangerous ones that get all the press; including the boomslang, the bite of which doesn't show its effects for many hours, when the victim begins to bleed from every body orifice, according to one book I read. The venom is a hemotoxin, meaning that it disables the blood-clotting process. The shredded skin of a boomslang is one of the ingredients of "polyjuice potion" in J.K. Rowling's novel *Harry Potter and the Chamber of Secrets*.

Rural South African villagers burn all the dead grass in their villages every fall in a ritual similar to the "field burning" that takes place each year in Western Oregon when farmers burn their grass-seed fields to rid them of pests. I asked several Zulus why the grass is burned and each answer was a variation of, "I don't know; we've always done it." I suspect that at one point, many hundreds of years ago, maybe thousands, it was to rid the villages of snakes. Maybe it still is. Snakes are still seen occasionally in villages, but usually in "the bush" outside populated areas. I suppose that would justify burning the grass, since there didn't seem to be many snakes in the villages, but it seemed odd that no one knew the origin of the practice. Zulus also love to sweep dirt. At most village homes all vegetation had been removed for many feet away on all sides of the home, and sometimes all the way to the road. I suspect this was another measure to keep snakes away from the house. Most homeowners kept that dirt swept the same way a compulsive American would sweep his porch daily, or a housewife would vacuum her carpet with regularity.

Mdu told me he had seen both a large cobra and a long mamba on separate occasions while swimming in a river in a remote area not far from Goodhome, when he was about fifteen. He said he was snoozing in the sun and awakened to see the mamba coiled next to him, mere inches away. He moved away slowly and the snake slithered off in the other direction. It might seem odd to many Westerners that black South Africans have such notions about snakes, but it isn't really all that different than American wives' tales about black cats, not walking under ladders, breaking mirrors, or throwing salt over one's shoulder.

21

How Do You Say 'Fuck You' in Zulu?

Unlike Oregon, South Africa is near the equator, and there isn't much difference between summer and winter, in terms of when it gets light and dark. Most South Africans don't even recognize spring and fall. They think in terms of summer and winter. At the height of summer in the Pacific Northwest it stays light until about 9:30 p.m., offering several more hours a day to engage in favorite summertime activities. Light comes about 5 a.m. In the depths of winter Oregonians can expect it to get dark about 4:30 p.m. and not see sunrise the next morning until about 7:30. But in Goodhome in summer, first light came about 6 a.m. and darkness about 6:30 p.m., give or take thirty minutes difference in winter. Temperatures were not extreme because we were in the foothills of a mountain range. Summertime highs were rarely above eighty or eighty-five (F) and though there were many cold winter mornings when it dipped into the high twenties or low thirties, most of the time it was in the forties or fifties. Thanks to the British influence, South Africans use the metric system and measure temperatures in Celsius so that whenever I talked temperatures with locals I had to apply the formula that would let me roughly convert Fahrenheit degrees into Celsius. There was no built-in indoor heat in most village homes—though some people had small electric space heaters. Whatever temperature it was outside it was the same or only slightly warmer inside. Walls were made of cinderblocks, mud or stucco, with no insulation. Warmth came from heavy blankets or sharing one's bed with another person. I had heavy blankets.

I also had mice in mid-winter for several weeks. I couldn't find snap traps that are popular in the U.S.—and more humane than poison—so I had my daughter send me a few. Meantime I wondered if the mice were as cold as I was and would want to share my bed. They were big mice, double the size of Oregon's wild version, and they ran around the rafters every night. They also would scurry across the floor, or hide in the small couch in the kitchen/living area, burrowing into the stuffing. The cinderblock homes have no ceilings, only rafters topped by a corrugated metal roof. One night I decided to fight back and threw shoes at the mice as they raced over head. I tried seven times to nail one of them, but never came close. When I finally started to win the rodent war I posted the news on Facebook:

"Rodent vs. Man—Score: Gary 1; rodents 0. I've won the first battle with the mice that invaded my home about two weeks ago and thwarted my efforts to reclaim my privacy. Regrettably, I had to use poison pellets instead of a mousetrap, which I believe would have been more humane. But I couldn't find one in four or five stores where I checked, and some people didn't know what I was talking about when I asked. He was a worthy and stalwart opponent. I thought he would die in his nest buried deep in one of the ratty love seats I have, and would smell for weeks as he decomposed. But, when I got home yesterday, there he was, stone cold dead in the middle of the floor. Fat little bugger, too. He ate well for two weeks, grabbing all the bait I left out for him, while escaping my creative jury-rigged traps. In the end, I saluted him smartly and sincerely before

I tossed his cold, stiff carcass into the burn barrel!"

Eventually I got rid of four of them, only to then find a baby toad (the Zulu word is *xoxo*, which calls for two clicks of the tongue to pronounce it correctly) that had slipped under the door during a rainstorm. He was about the size of a quarter, much smaller than the adult versions that were often about after rain. Adult toads were the size of a toddler's fist and no doubt ate many bugs, including spiders, which I like. As long as the spiders built their webs in a corner or high out of reach, I let them be. I kept the toad in a big pickle jar for several weeks with water and small rocks, named it Crouton and fed it flies. I turned it loose when I had to go to Pretoria for several days. I saw rats several times, outside, going through the trash, but never inside. The Zulu word for rat, or mouse, is *igundwane* (ee-goon-DWAN-nay).

I had more rainy days than sunny in the time I lived in Goodhome and worked at Masiphile. Nearly as much in summer as in winter, though it was warmer in the summer. Once, unusually, there were six inches of snow (though Zungu exaggerated like my five-year-old grandnephew might, and claimed it was a foot). Rain was often accompanied by thunder and lightning. Many was the time my three-minute walk from the main dirt road, after leaving the taxi, was through heavy rain, thunder and lightning strikes uncomfortably close. Often, especially in summer, the day would start without a cloud in the sky, with temps in the 60s. It would stay that way for several hours, and then get warmer, tricking me into believing it would be pleasant all day. Lunch might be outside in the warm sunshine. Then about one p.m. white fluffy clouds would start to roll in from the direction of the Indian Ocean. By three or so they would turn gray or black and by four it would be raining, or we'd have a hail storm with stones the size of marbles. I learned to always carry my rain jacket, no matter the weather in the morning. Not long before I returned I read that a family of four, parents and two young children, had been killed when they were struck by lightning while walking across a field near Pietermaritzburg, about an hour south of Estcourt. Such stories were common.

Nearly as common were the stories about horrible traffic accidents. Ten children had been killed when the bakkie they were riding in swerved to miss a cow, struck a bridge and sailed into a river; eighteen farm workers on the back of a flatbed truck were killed when the driver tried, and failed, to beat a train—limbs and body parts littering the highway. Taxis might collide head-on on a rural highway, or in a city, when one blew a stop sign, killing many. I read that South Africa has the highest traffic fatality rate in the world. Poor enforcement, poor roads, poorly maintained vehicles and fatalistic attitudes about life no doubt all contribute to the high accident rate. Back in training Minky told me that when livestock on the road cause an accident it was the owner of the animal who was responsible for the damage. I found this interesting since the opposite is true in much of the Western U.S. where livestock have the right-of-way—at least in rural areas identified as "open range." If a steer is struck by a driver's car, the driver must reimburse the rancher.

Over the years, many Peace Corps volunteers have died in traffic accidents, many of them in Africa, though none while I was there, that I was aware of. In training, while lecturing about the Peace Corps policy that prohibits hitchhiking, a staff member told the story of when four Peace Corps volunteers in an African country—not South Africa—accepted a ride from a stranger who turned out to be drunk. Once they realized this, they asked him to let them out, but he refused to stop. Later, he crashed the car and two of the four volunteers were killed, the others badly injured.

I have my own close-call stories to tell, as do most of my SA25 colleagues, I imagine. Paige from Eastern Washington and I made a presentation about the Volunteer Support Network, during training for SA26 (three Oregonians in that group, too). Afterward, Franz, one of the drivers, took us, along with Arlene, the medical officer, in a Peace Corps vehicle to Pietermaritzburg to drop Paige at the taxi rank so she could catch a taxi back to her village. The rest of us would return to Pretoria, a five-hour drive. Arlene would go back to medical work and I would return to the U.S. for Christmas 2012. We were just north of the city, stuck in a slow-moving lane for trucks. Franz had started to move over to the next lane when he heard a blast from a truck horn. He turned just in time to see and react to a huge semi, barreling along in the same lane, downhill. Franz reacted and hit the brakes as the truck, loaded and probably weighing forty tons, sailed past us, horn still blaring to warn other drivers. He missed us by inches. His brakes clearly had failed and he was trying to maintain control, warn other drivers, and not hit another vehicle. We could smell the burning brakes.

I wonder if the outcome would have been different if we'd had a different driver, whose reflexes might not have been as quick as Franz's. If we'd been sitting in the middle of that lane—where we would have been one second later if Franz hadn't braked so quickly—we'd have been hit by an 80,000-pound truck going eighty miles an hour. We'd have been toast. A couple miles further the highway leveled out and the truck was able to coast to a stop, brakes smoking like a slow-burning Oregon forest fire.

At the training where Paige and I had just spoken, people had called to me from the back of the room to say,

"Speak up, we can't hear you." A few months later I would learn that one of the symptoms of Parkinson's is a softening of the voice—because the muscles that control the vocal chords are affected, causing people to ask you to speak louder. The night before, Arlene and I had gone to the hotel bar for a drink and to talk about my first book, which she had read, a novel about mental illness loosely-based on my career. She shared her own story about when she was a Peace Corps medical officer in a different African country and had to escort a psychotic volunteer home to the U.S. They had passed through two different African airports without security authorities finding the foot-long knife the young woman had hidden in her carry-on luggage. It wasn't until after they landed in Atlanta that the knife was discovered. Also in the bar that night was a thirty-five-ish teacher named Vanessa who convinced three young Afrikaner men that the scar on her stomach that she showed them came from an encounter with a lion, which she disabled, she said, by poking it in the eye with a pen. One of her friends backed her up by telling the men, "She's a teacher, she's always prepared!" I think it was just a story Vanessa made up—but I wasn't sure.

We dropped Paige at the rank and the rest of us settled in for the long ride back to post. Arlene and I dozed off. About three or four hours into the trip we were awakened by a loud crash. A softball-sized object, a rock, or a chunk of tire from a passing truck bounced into the windshield, leaving a round, basketball-sized crack inches away from Franz's face. He was traveling about seventy miles, or eighty-five kilometers, an hour. If any number of variables had been a little different—if we'd been going a little faster, or the shape of the object had been different, or if the windshield hadn't been high quality shatter-proof glass—the outcome could have been tragic. For the second time that day we looked at one another, laughed nervously, and, in my case, breathed a short prayer of thanks. And stopped wondering if it was really true that South Africa has the highest per capita traffic fatality rate in the world. A few months later, Ashley from Chicago told us that seven high school learners in her town were walking home from school when they were struck by a car driven by a drunk driver. Three were killed, the others badly injured.

The rest of the trip was uneventful and a few hours later I was winging my way home for Christmas. Masiphile was closed for a long holiday break and I had a chance to see family and friends. My friend Nel in Eugene arranged a party for me so I could see everyone at once, rather than have fifty individual coffee dates. She suggested we ask everyone to bring something that was needed in Africa, so I suggested items for a first-aid kit—bandages, tweezers, scissors, adhesive tape, antibiotic ointment, rubber gloves. My friends were generous and I put together two excellent kits, one for Masiphile and the other claimed by Julie from Rochester for her organization in Limpopo Province. When I brought the new kit in one morning not long after I got back, Nonhlanhla screamed, ran around her desk and threw her arms around me. Turned out that such a kit was one of the requirements the provincial Department of Social Services had made at the last inspection. Who knew Band-Aids could be so exciting? The trip home for Christmas cost $2,000-plus in airfare, but it was nice to see everyone, especially my dog, Carly, who went bananas. She had been living with Megan's family. Of course, if I'd known then that in just three short months I would be leaving Peace Corps and returning for good, I would not have come home in December.

The trip back to Goodhome the first week in January 2013 had been uneventful until the end. It was an all-day series of taxi rides: Pretoria to Ladysmith, Ladysmith to Estcourt, and then the local taxi to the village. It was just before seven p.m. when the taxi from Ladysmith pulled into the rank. It was dark but for one vehicle, which was about to pull away. I ran, lugging three bags, and got there just in time to catch it. Miraculously, it was headed for Goodhome; the last taxi of the night. I stowed my bags and wedged myself in-between two men, drunken friends, each drinking a can of beer, common practice in Africa. They offered to share their beer but I declined.

At the edge of town the driver stopped for petrol. While the tank was being filled, one of the passengers got out to chat with a friend. The gas tank full, the driver drove away, leaving the passenger behind, speaking to his friend. Several other passengers yelled that the young man running after the taxi was one of us, but the driver ignored them and kept driving. We were a couple of kilometers out of town when the driver's cell phone rang. It was the owner of the taxi, according to one of my eavesdropping seatmates, who had been called by the man left at the petrol station. The driver pulled over to the shoulder and engaged in a heated conversation with the owner. I could tell from the driver's voice and demeanor, and the way he walked, that he was drunk. Some of us got out to stretch our legs, listen to the angry driver, and take care of business in the nearby tall grass. It began to rain.

Finally, the driver finished his phone call, we all got back into the taxi, and headed down the road to Goodhome. The man left behind was out of luck. At that point, I could have chosen to not return to the taxi, since the driver was in no condition to drive safely, but the alternative was to be standing next to a busy highway with no shoulders and no light, at night, in the rain, lugging two heavy bags and a briefcase, holding a computer worth more than most rural South Africans earned in a year. I was at least fifteen kilometers from the village. There would be no more taxis until morning. It was the kind of situation we had discussed many times in training—which choice of multiple bad ones to choose. I chose to stay with the taxi. At some point, the passenger in the front seat next to the driver left and the driver invited an attractive woman in the back to take that seat. She did. The driver, flirting with the woman, drove unsafely, speeding and weaving along, dropping passengers at their stops, for the next twenty minutes until, finally, we were in Goodhome—and still alive. He turned off the main tar road to the dirt road that led to my stop, two kilometers down. Three young men got out leaving only me and the woman in the front. The driver drove on a short distance, stopped and ordered me to get out.

"I don't get out for two more kilometers," I told him.

"Get out now!" he thundered.

"I'm not getting out; you have to take me to the white church."

"No! Out!"

"I paid for the whole ride. I'm not getting out here. You have to take me two more kilometers."

He said something I couldn't understand, and then was done arguing. He turned into a driveway and backed up, turning around to head back the way he had come. I saw the writing on the wall and envisioned having to walk many more kilometers, in the dark, in the rain, lugging three bags. I capitulated. "Ok, ok," I told him. "I'll get out." I did, and as he drove away, I yelled, as loud as I could, "How do you say 'fuck you' in Zulu," a phrase I had learned at IST one night over beers, but had forgotten since I hadn't had a chance to use it. I also had learned how to say fuck you in Russian—"Yeb vas!"—but that wouldn't have served me in a Zulu village. The driver kept going. I didn't think he heard me. The three young men who had disembarked just before me had been walking in my direction and had seen and heard the exchange between me and the driver. When I asked the driver how to say fuck you in Zulu, they laughed, then offered to help me carry my bags the last two kilometers. I gave them each five rand.

22

Taxis: A Culture of Their Own

Few things will slow down a rural South African taxi driver. A speed bump is one of them. I speculate that most drivers don't own the vehicles they drive. A fleet of taxis in a particular area probably is owned by a person who is pretty well off. If a hired driver causes damage to the taxi he probably will have to pay for repairs. Hitting a speed bump at high speed could pop a tire, mess up a transaxle, throw the vehicle out of alignment, knock a hole in an oil pan and/or cause loss of control. It wouldn't cause the damage hitting a 2,000-pound steer would (which happens occasionally), but hitting a speed bump is still something drivers should avoid.

There are lots of speed bumps in the rural area southwest of Estcourt. Some are in places one would expect to find them: near schools, cattle crossings (actually, cattle can cross anywhere, since most are not fenced in), municipal offices or businesses; neighborhoods with children, clinics with foot traffic, and before blind rises or blind curves. Other times you find them in the middle of nowhere, places where you wouldn't expect them.

I learned a lot about taxis and taxi culture in Africa, but perhaps one of the most interesting was something we learned in training. When a taxi driver sees a hitchhiker, who he thinks is cutting into his income, he will call other drivers on his cell phone. The drivers meet where the hitchhiker is, jump out of their taxis, surround the person and force him into a vehicle. They then take him back to the nearest rank and order him to take a taxi instead of hitch-hiking. In America, we would call this kidnapping or un-lawful imprisonment, major felonies that could net you ten to twenty years in the slammer. But in South Africa, free enterprise! I found it hard to believe, but, they told us this in official Peace Corps training, so it must be true. I never witnessed it, nor meet anyone who had. Thankfully, I never had to hitchhike in an emergency.

Occasionally I did accept a ride from a village neighbor or someone else I knew. One day I stayed later than usual at Masiphile because one of the Peace Corps drivers, AB—who had brought me to Estcourt in the beginning—was deliver-ing a truckload of things that another volunteer, Peggie from Southern California, was donating to Masiphile because she had to leave for family reasons. We were pretty close and I was excited when she gave us bedding, clothing, kitchen gear, non-perishable food, towels and toys and lots of other useful things. It was after five o'clock by the time we finished unloading the truck and I waved good-bye to the driver and started down to the main road to flag a taxi. When I got home I learned that Spamondla, or "Spa," Mr. Zungu's twenty-eight-year-old nephew, had crashed his truck on the main road, having taken a curve too fast. He had picked up six or seven high school students and a friend, and was driv-ing them to Goodhome so they wouldn't have to walk in the rain. Most were in the canopy-covered back.

It's highly probable that Spa would have seen me and offered me a ride. I would have accepted. Fortunately, a guardian angel was watching over all of us—me by delaying my departure from Masiphile, and all those students and friends. No one was seriously hurt, including Spa, though he was sporting a black eye, bruises, a nasty cut on his forehead, and a limp. In the U.S. the truck would have been hauled to a junkyard and replaced by the insurance company. But not in rural South Africa. I doubt Spa had insurance, and a couple of days later all the Zungu men gathered around the wrecked bakkie, kicking the tires, pulling off bent fenders and discussing how they could salvage the truck. So much for free "taxi" rides by Spa, at least for a time.

A few years ago I participated in the "citizens' police academy," a ten-week opportunity for ordinary citizens in Eugene. Once a week for three hours of lecture and Saturday field trips to the crime lab and the firing range we learned what cops really do, and why. The personnel director told us that the ability to multi-task is one of the most important traits the city looks for in would-be officers. Many people are not good multi-taskers.

But you should see a South African taxi driver: he can drive sixty miles an hour on curvy mountain roads with no shoulders, accept money and make change, tinker with the radio or stereo (after thumbing through his CD collection), honk his horn, shift gears, talk to the guy next to him, wave at friends, watch for cattle, goats, chickens and kids (and swerve around them if necessary), pass other vehicles, dodge potholes, listen for passengers yelling where they want to get out, flirt with the attractive woman behind him, watch the mirror (if he has one), tell a drunk to behave, watch the roadside for people flagging him down, and turn on the windshield wipers, heater or anything else with a switch. Sometimes he even converses, in English, with the local Peace Corps volunteer. And if his cell phone rings? He always answers it like any typical black South African. If you're in his taxi, you better hope he's a good multi-tasker and that it's your lucky day. Maybe he'd make a good police officer.

Sometimes the driver gets help from the person in the front passenger seat next to him when it comes to collecting money and making change. It's customary for that person to assist the driver so he has one less thing to worry about. On one trip to town, I was in the back row on the right side. I had exact change for the twelve-rand ride. I passed that to the guy on my left, who also had exact change. He passed both of our fares to the woman to his left, who also had exact change, and she passed all of it to the woman to her left, who had a fifty-rand note.

The total now for the four of us was forty-eight rand. She kept all the money from the first three of us and passed the fifty forward, telling the person, "four," meaning money for four passengers. That woman also had exact change, so she handed her two-rand coin back to the woman in my row, leaving sixty remaining, which she passed to the next woman, saying, "five." The money went forward, the driver got sixty rand, exact change for five passengers, and didn't have to make change. This is a simplified example, since at that point there were still ten people, further forward, who hadn't paid. Some of those may also have had bigger bills that needed changing, hopefully before money got to the driver, or his assistant. I was that person, a nervous one, in the front passenger seat a couple of times. It's a big responsibility, since you have to make sure no one gets ripped off—driver or any passenger.

Most taxis are minibuses—similar to those old VW minibuses hippies used to drive in the 1960s—but bigger. Many are Toyota products. The top-of-the-line model is the Quantum (it's also what Peace Corps vans are). All are "certified" for anywhere from thirteen to sixteen passengers, depending on the model. Goats and chickens and fifty-kilogram bags of maize or flour aren't part of the legal capacity. In the local villages, drivers loaded up with as many passengers as possible. Most trips are local, to schools, the clinic or, in my case, the organization where I volunteered. There are periodic traffic stops on the main roads by municipal or provincial traffic officers who enforce the rules about passenger capacity, equipment like lights and turn signals in working order, proper paperwork. The driver's goal is to offload as many passengers as necessary to reach his certification number before he comes to a police stop. Seatbelts were usually disabled or missing, except for the front passenger and driver seats. I was in taxis a couple of times that were overloaded as we approached a police traffic stop, causing the driver to order two or three standing passengers to get down on their knees and hide, thus successfully avoiding a possible citation.

All the taxis I saw in my southern KwaZulu-Natal area had stickers that read "Nooduitgang," which is "Emergency Exit" in Afrikaans. I found this annoying since 99.999 percent of taxi passengers in my area were Zulu or other black Africans, not Afrikaner. I supposed this had more to do with the cities where taxis are manufactured or sold than it did with any conscious plan to confuse passengers. No one but me seemed to care.

Here's a riddle: When does two equal three? The answer is, when one taxi on a two-lane road wants to pass another vehicle and needs the assistance of an on-coming taxi, which means that three vehicles need to occupy two lanes, at the same time, side by side, while all are going about eighty kilometers per hour. This calls for some skilled and astute choreography. The oncoming taxi moves to his left, straddling the edge of the pavement, while the car being passed straddles the center line. For about two or three seconds the vehicles are side by side, mere inches away from one another, until the pass is complete, whereupon all return to their lanes, life goes on and breathing resumes.

Countrywide, I would guess there are several crashes a week, but few of them fatal. On the other hand, the taxi is the primary form of transportation in South Africa, where most people can't afford to own cars. I once heard that there are 30,000 taxis in Durban alone. Imagine how many there are throughout KZN; in the entire country. So, statistically, even if you held your breath and feared for your life every time you got into a taxi, you weren't likely to die on any particular trip.

And me? I was once in a bus that crashed and rolled in the mountains of Mexico at night. I only sustained minor injuries. My theory is that the powers that be assign no more than one Third World, public transport crash per person, per lifetime. And I'd already had mine!

Taxi drivers, like most black South Africans, love their music. Their vehicles are equipped with CD players, some of which accept thumb drives in lieu of CDs. They play music loudly, often African or Western tunes, blues, rock and roll or spiritual. Some are more eclectic than others. My favorite driver in the village, Gijimani ("fast runner" in Zulu), was playing a classic fifties Hank Williams country tune, "Your Cheatin' Heart," the first time I rode in his taxi. He offered me free rides a couple of times when he was headed home for the night, saw me walking, and was no longer on duty. On one trip in Gijimani's taxi, from Estcourt to Imbabazane on a warm Saturday afternoon, I was in the rear seat, subject to serious bouncing when the vehicle hit a pothole or a speed bump. Ouch. On my left were two loud but friendly drunks, polishing off a large bottle of beer, and on my right a woman with a baby. Five of us in a seat designed for three. The woman began to breastfeed her crying baby, which of course bothered no one because this was Zulu country in rural South Africa. It reminded of the time when my daughter was kicked out of a café in a small community near Eugene for breastfeeding one of my grandchildren. The U.S. is not always ahead of developing countries.

Taxis were often decorated with Bible verses or ads for companies like "dearmomma.com," a catering service. Once I posted a picture of one of the Goodhome taxis on Facebook to see if anyone recognized Exodus 20:2-17, the Ten Commandants. The reference was painted on the taxi's front. I think my niece, Jessica, correctly answered that brain teaser.

But the most amazing taxi story I heard was the one published in the Peace Corps South Africa monthly newsletter written by Gary and Meredith Gaffney of SA24 about an experience their twenty-three-year-old son, Devon, had when he came to visit. They called it "The Unexpected Taxi Driver," which I've paraphrased:

Devon did some traveling on his own until his parents were free to visit and one day, traveling in Limpopo, he found himself sitting in a taxi with just the driver and one other passenger. When the time came to embark on the journey, the driver asked whether Devon thought he could drive the taxi. Since Devon grew up in a state where some rural kids drive at fourteen, he said, "Sure". The driver handed over the keys and away they went with this young American driving the South African taxi through rural Limpopo. Devon enjoyed his taxi driving stint and said it was hilarious when he stopped to collect passengers, who did a double take when they saw the youthful, white driver. Eventually, everyone on the taxi was laughing and anticipating the fun of seeing the confusion, and then smiles, on the faces of incoming riders. After about forty kilometers the driver took back his taxi for the rest of the trip.

The second most interesting taxi story was my own adventure when I was trying to get to Ballito, a beach community north of Durban, for a Peace Corps volunteer-organized weekend event called a "provincial conference" that was as much social as it was educational. It wasn't required, but most of us were there. I left early that day since I had several taxi rides ahead of me. Still, I was the last person in the last taxi to Durban. I got to Durban about four in the afternoon and asked six or seven drivers where I could catch the taxi to Ballito. Not one had heard of the town. I concluded this was because Ballito was a beach town vacation spot for white people and it was no surprise that taxi drivers in Durban, even those who had been driving for years, had never heard of this city of five-million-rand homes.

Later, a Durban police officer saw me looking confused and asked me where I was from. When I told him I was from "near Estcourt," he smiled and said, in a loud voice, in somewhat exaggerated fashion, "I'm from Wembezi," a township midway between Estcourt and my collection of Imbabazane villages, a few kilometers from where I lived. When I told him I was trying to find the taxi to Ballito he instantly made it his mission to help me. There ensued a madcap race, like something one might see in a Charlie Chaplin movie, down busy streets, through packed markets, up stairways and down, around corners, across busy four-lane highways, leaping over guardrails. I struggled to keep up with him since I was lugging a duffel bag and he was unencumbered.

After we had gone a kilometer or two, he saw a taxi driver he seemed to know who told him how to get to the rank where the taxi to Ballito was located. I arrived a few seconds later, out of breath, just in time for the officer to more-or-less commandeer the taxi to take us the last kilometer to the magic spot. The policeman escorted me to the right taxi, put me in the front seat next to the driver, and told him to take good care of me. He laughed, poked me in the chest, and said, in perfect English, "You, sir, are a lucky man!" I laughed and said, "I know. Ngiyabonga." The rest of the ride was uneventful. I arrived about six, the last one to get there. I shared a room at the hostel with two young women from Netherlands who were also volunteers and I was able to talk with them about their country, since just a few months earlier, before I arrived in Africa, I had spent four days in Amsterdam. A few of us stayed over Sunday night at the Monkey Bay Backpacker (hostel) and had a braai (the Afrikaner word for BBQ), drank too much and played truth or dare. About midnight we made a pact that what happens in Ballito, stays in Ballito and toddled off to bed.

Six weeks later we were at a conference center in Pretoria for a few days of training when we heard that the legality of President Obama's healthcare legislation—the Affordable Care Act, or "Obamacare"—had been upheld, 5-4, by the Supreme Court. The liberal Democrats, most of us, gathered in the hotel bar that night and celebrated. The U.S. was one step closer to having a national health care plan almost as good as South Africa's. A few months later we were in Werner Beach, a different Durban area seaside town, to share Thanksgiving dinner. On the way back to Durban on Sunday, with Greg and Pat, the volunteer couple from Seattle, the train broke down and one hundred people had to transfer to buses.

23

Life with the Zungu Family

Most days when I got home I would visit with whoever was around. Often that was Hlonie (SHLO-nee), one of Zungu's nieces, who ran the household (Zungu had a wife, but she was a nurse who lived in Durban and came home on weekends only a couple of times while I lived there). Hlonie did all the laundry (though I did see Spa do his own a time or two, unusual because he was male), and all the shopping, cooking and cleaning. I did all my own laundry. More than once when I was gone Hlonie saw that rain was coming and took my dry laundry down, and put it on the couch for me. It wasn't unusual to come home and find someone on my couch, or evidence that someone had been there, even if I had locked the door. I suspect the spare key to my place hung on a hook in the main house, reachable to anyone who wanted to use it. It was the culture. Many people had a your-home-is-my-home attitude that most Americans would find disconcerting, but I accepted it. Once I came home after being gone for the weekend to find that there had been a large family gathering, including out of town guests, and Zungu had let an elderly relative sleep in my bed. The man was gone when I got there, but I knew he'd been there because he had made the bed and his dress shoes and nice jacket were laid out neatly nearby. Nothing was ever missing.

Often I would eat a PBJ sandwich and an apple in the early evening, and read for a while (I read more books in fourteen months than in the previous twenty-five years). For night time reading the place was equipped with forty-watt bulbs that weren't strong enough to read by, unless I stood on the bed, leaned against the cinderblock wall and held the book aloft, angled toward the light. But that was no fun. Before long I bought a nice reading lamp, which was immeasurably better, but only worked when there was power. When power was out I read by "torch".

Other days I would prepare tea for Hlonie and me. She deserved it, and I was trying to model appropriate behavior for Zulu men used to having Zulu women wait on them. Hlonie was about thirty years old and had a boyfriend in Durban. She wore a patch over one eye, the result of a jealous woman throwing acid in her face. I asked her about it once and she told me that the woman believed, incorrectly, that she was having an affair with her boyfriend. Hlonie made several trips to Durban for medical treatment during the time I lived there. She explained that, eventually, skin grafts would replace the damaged skin and she would be able to lose the patch. I gathered that this treatment was covered by the government since South Africa, unlike the U.S., has a national health plan that ensures that all, including the poorest, have access to medical care.

Another of Zungu's nieces, Ntokozo ("joy" in Zulu), who was Sendile's sister, stayed with us after she had a baby. The baby never left the house for a month. I never learned the baby girl's name, but Joy told me it meant "well and carefully planned" in Zulu. I told her about Peace Corps and why I was in Goodhome. She implored me to "tell people in America how difficult Africans' lives are." She was one of many people who specifically talked about water issues, describing the time a year before when the family had a memorial service for her mother (whose grave was outside my door), and there was not enough water to accommodate the guests.

Often various neighbors from across the street or around the village would stop by to visit. All were friendly and treated me well. Occasionally, one would ask me for a few rand, but, in keeping with Peace Corps recommendations, I always told them what I told every panhandler: "Sorry, I don't have any rand I can give away today." It didn't make sense to say I didn't have any money; people would have known that was a lie. People were always accepting of my response, never becoming angry or threatening. I never once felt fearful, even when I went out at night to get water, or walk up the road to Mdu's house, or for better cell phone reception to call my mother or Sindisiwe. At least once a week at night, sometimes late, groups of people would walk by, singing, often religious songs. Other times bakkies with loudspeakers and signs would drive back and forth on the dirt roads, shouting news about upcoming community political events.

Peace Corps volunteers generally negotiate various things with the families they live with, often to include having dinner with the family, if not every day, then maybe a couple of days a week. I never dined with Zungu's family, though there were occasions when someone would deliver plates of food for me when I got home, after being gone. I preferred to prepare my own food, even when it meant more PBJ or a can of cold beans if the power was out.

Spa was the designated fixer of things around the compound, including trying to keep me in power. He'd had some training in carpentry and had a set of tools. When the power went out it was usually restored within a few hours or a day or two, though twice I was without power for thirteen days. Sometimes it was the weather, other times it was the funky wiring. Of course, I only had power at all because of the chunk of concrete I had to balance atop the plug, attached to a power strip plugged into the wall in the bedroom. It was the only outlet that worked, which meant the bedroom was also the kitchen. One time Spa determined that the problem seemed to be a connection that was about ten feet off the floor in the common area. They didn't have a ladder, which I found odd for a family complex of half an acre, many trees, and four buildings. But rural South Africans are masters of flexibility, innovation, jury-rigging fixes and making do with what they have. I saw tractors like the one my grand-father had in the 1950s that, I'd bet, had had their motors or transmissions rebuilt a dozen times to prolong their lives for another season. And everyone's an amateur electrician. Spa moved the couch to a point below where he needed to work, set my one dining chair atop the couch, then put an empty five-gallon bucket, upside down, on the chair. He then climbed to the top, stood on tiptoes and, with tools in each hand, worked on the connection while the whole con-traption swayed back and forth as he worked, threatening to topple the whole business to the concrete floor. It was a per-formance worthy of a circus. When he'd fixed the problem he leaped down, put the "ladder" parts back in place, and I was able to cook my dinner.

Though everyone at Zungu's compound treated me nicely, my housing always felt a little tenuous because once Zungu agreed I could live there, it still remained for him and Nonhlanhla to negotiate the terms. The housing itself was offered for free, but, typically, a volunteer would pay some-thing for the electricity, maybe 100-150 rand per month, about twelve dollars. And typically Peace Corps would pay for the installation of "burglar bars" over the windows, and install metal security doors over the wooden ones. But Zungu and Nonhlanhla were both quite busy procrastinators and a bit passive-aggressive—especially Nonhlanhla. In the year I lived there they never managed to get together, by phone or in person, to work out the terms. They would not return one another's phone calls for months at a time, or one wouldn't be there when the other unexpectedly stopped by to talk. Each would complain mildly to me about the other, and I would deliver messages that never seemed to accomplish much.

On at least three occasions I tried to negotiate directly with Zungu about the terms of my stay there, offering to pay for the power, but he wouldn't discuss it with me, insisting that he could discuss it only with Nonhlanhla because it was she who had made the agreement with him. One time he said the reason for Nonhlanhla's lack of contact was that she was ill or under a lot of stress because of her many responsibilities. A couple of times he seemed so frustrated I feared he might decide the only solution was for him to tell me to move, but, fortunately, it never came to that. Not all volunteers were so fortunate, some finding themselves hanging out at one of the backpackers near post in Pretoria for weeks while staff looked for new housing. Rarely, if ever, was the loss of housing the result of something the volunteer said or did. Rather, cultural issues, such as people coming into your room when you weren't there, were the problem. Or one side or the other had expectations of the arrangement that were too far apart to work out.

On one of my afternoon visits with Hlonie, we were joined by her mother, who, I thought, lived nearby in Goodhome. She knew who I was, though we had not previously met, and greeted me by saying (I thought), "I'm going to be a grandmother."

"Congratulations," I responded. "I'm a grandfather, three times," I said, holding up three fingers.

Days went by and one morning I saw Hlonie throwing up next to the latrine. "Ah, morning sickness," I presumed.

Later that day I saw her again and said, "I congratulated your mother the other day, but I never congratulated you." She looked puzzled. I told her I had seen her getting sick that morning and I mentioned "morning sickness." She was more confused. Turned out she wasn't pregnant, that her "mother" was really her grandmother and was merely introducing herself to me as such, not saying, "I'm going to be a grandmother." Whoops!

Village life on the weekends was a different story. Most Saturdays, after sleeping in a bit, I made the twelve-rand, twenty-five-kilometer trip to Estcourt to shop for supplies, maybe have a restaurant meal, get a haircut, pick up my mail at the post office, meet friends or otherwise do something different than what I did Monday through Friday. It wasn't *necessary* to go to town every week, but I liked the change of pace and the chance to learn more about the culture and interact with locals, including the few whites who lived there. Often I had breakfast at a chicken franchise called Baricela's while I read one of the Durban papers—or the local Estcourt paper—to catch up on the crime news. In addition to other local fast food outlets, Estcourt had McDonald's, KFC, Carl's Jr and a couple others that Americans would recognize. Or, after shopping I would go to The Village Gossip, the coffee shop next to the Thyme and Again B&B, where I had stayed my first night in town after training. I presume both were owned by whites, though I never met the owners; all the staff was black. The coffee shop served great coffee and desserts and it was often my last stop before heading for the rank to catch a taxi back to Goodhome.

Some Saturdays I hit the library, which had free Wi-Fi, or the computer store to check email if there had been bad reception at Masiphile the day before. It cost fifteen rand, about $1.50, for thirty minutes.

Miyobongwe (me-yo-BONE-gway), who cut my hair every couple of months, was one of my favorite town people. One of the Masiphile volunteers who accompanied me to town one day introduced us. Miyobongwe often went by "My-be" since whites and other non-blacks, such as the Indians, had trouble pronouncing his name. I didn't. He was friendly and outgoing and often wore pink or lavender shirts, though I never made assumptions about his sexual orientation. He employed several local black women to wash hair, assist him, or do intricate braiding. He spoke English well and told me he had grown up in Estcourt, and had worked in salons in Johannesburg, Durban and Pietermaritzburg before returning to his home town to open his own shop. He charged thirty rand, about three bucks, to cut my hair and trim my beard. There were also street vendors who cut hair using clippers hooked up to car batteries for power. They charged ten rand, about a dollar, but one had to wonder about the cleanliness and safety of their instruments.

I also got to know an Indian man who ran one of the pharmacies. I never learned his name, but he expressed an interest in my mission and donated a box of rubber gloves to Masiphile when I told him of the need. I learned early on that most businesses were owned by whites, mostly Afrikaners, I supposed, or Indians or Pakistanis. Most of the grocery stores downtown were owned by non-blacks who were Muslims, and didn't sell alcohol. But, oddly, they sold cigarettes. I had to walk a mile or so to the Spar, a national grocery chain, to buy the occasional bottle of wine. I sometimes called it the "white side of town." It literally was on the other side of the railroad tracks from Mackson's, where I usually shopped, and which had two stores, one at each end of downtown. Most Spar shoppers were white or Coloured, while I was often one of only a few whites at the larger stores in the center of town where the black locals shopped, and where prices were lower. Before long I lowered my wine-drinking standards and traded bottles for boxes. One box held the same amount as three bottles of wine, yet weighed not much more and cost less, sixty-nine rand, about seven dollars, to thirty rand, about three dollars, for a bottle. I cut the empty boxes in half and used them for things like silverware trays or storing medicines. I drank my wine discreetly from an old blue tin camping cup I brought from home.

On one of my first Saturday shopping trips I was standing in front of Mackson's and was nearly bowled over by a shoplifter being chased by two security guards, armed not with guns, but with nightsticks (or maybe they were three-foot lengths of rubber hose). The first guard tackled the thief when he was about a foot away from me, brought him down to the pavement, as the second guard arrived. He began beating the young man on the backs of his legs, though the man was restrained and not resisting. I leaped out of the way. In the U.S. such behavior by police officers or guards might get them in trouble with internal affairs, but not, apparently, in South Africa. The guards dragged the perpetrator toward the front door of the store, but stopped to again whack him several more times, though he still wasn't resisting. All of this was witnessed by more than fifty people, and across the street from the police station. I wondered if the next step was to call the police so the man could be arrested, or whether the guards' street justice was the end of it.

On weekends in downtown Estcourt the streets were crowded with vendors selling just about anything imaginable: jewelry, new and used clothing, fruit and vegetables, shoes, traditional Zulu clothing and headgear, pencils, wallets and trinkets and belts, art, chicken feed, CDs, stereos, brooms, underwear and socks, cow heads (boil off the hide and make stew), bedding, some of it made on the spot by old women using antique sewing machines with foot pedals or hand-operated handles. Huge, soft and decorative blankets—more like comforters—are a traditional Zulu gift to a newly married couple. I bought one—150 rand, about fifteen dollars—and it kept me warm on the coldest of winter nights. I was sorry I had to leave it behind, but it was too big to fit in my suitcase or carry on the plane. Many vendors had stands, but others walked around hawking their wares and describing them out loud like vendors at a baseball game or a rodeo.

One day I bought a doo-dad for thirty rand, about three dollars, the name of which I never learned. The cinderblock house I lived in was built in a hole and had no foundation. The device I bought would fill up the half-inch of space under the door and kept mice, spiders and snakes, and most of the muddy rain out. The house was one of those more-or-less identical structures, built by the government when apartheid ended, to help improve the lives of rural families all over South Africa. It baffled me that the people who had built so many houses, hundreds of thousands, in terrain that had been dug and scraped clean leaving bare, banked slopes surrounding the construction site—in an area with frequent heavy rain—never learned the importance of drainage. The first time my house flooded, I came home to find about two inches of water covering the floor, in every room. Hlonie and Spa helped me clean it up. A bunch of stuff was ruined, but nothing critical except my Zulu-English Dictionary. I propped the pages open in the sun to dry, two or three at a time over two weeks. The salvage operation was successful. After that I stacked important things on top of blocks, cardboard boxes, or the bed while I was away. The doo-dad I bought was often supplemented by a large, orange folded beach towel. The two "dams" kept out most of the water.

I often bought bananas, apples, pears and peaches from a woman who had a sidewalk stand outside the market. The manager didn't seem to mind the competition, even though her fruit was cheaper. I posted her picture on Facebook, after asking her permission. One Saturday I spent twenty rand to have my crumbling sandals sewed back together by a shoe-repair vendor, and his six-year-old son. Some of the things for sale on the street were items that would be illegal to sell in the U.S.: home-made hard liquor, moonshine, in reused bottles that probably came from someone's trash; and "cures" for AIDS and cancer that in the U.S. would catch the attention of the Food and Drug Administration. Nonhlanhla was especially incensed by such snake-oil salespeople, given Masiphile's mission of appropriately helping those deathly ill with HIV/AIDS, for which there is no cure. I won't repeat what she said should happen to such people, but it wasn't pretty. There were also small shops, one of which was a shoe store called the "Hike Store," whose emblem in the window looked suspiciously like a well-known symbol of an iconic athletic apparel company based in Oregon.

Most Saturdays I stood in the ATM line at First National Bank to get cash for shopping, often with forty or fifty other people, a twenty-minute wait. Everyone except me was black. Security guards, some wearing bullet-proof armor and with semi-automatic rifles, watched over some banks. My bank was closed at one point when an armed gang blew up several ATMs in the middle of the night and made off with what I suppose was a lot of money. It took two weeks to make repairs while the bank remained closed. One Saturday a rowdy parade of African National Congress elected officials and their supporters marched into the heart of the city. My friend Mkhize, the ward councilor, was in front, waving a sign and leading hundreds of people in rousing political songs. When he saw me he smiled, trotted over and shook my hand. I nervously looked around for photographers. It wouldn't do to have a picture of a Peace Corps volunteer on the front page of the local paper cozying up to a member of the ANC or any other political party in front of hundreds of locals. Peace Corps, rightfully, prides itself on its neutrality. Its credibility could be damaged if it were seen as favoring one party over another. In training we were told the story of a volunteer who wrote something critical of the party in office. Word of it got back to the South African government, which then complained to the U.S. Embassy. The volunteer was "administratively separated," a fancy term for getting fired. It mattered not one whit that every word the volunteer said was true. John, the country director, made it clear on more than one occasion that there would be zero tolerance for compromising Peace Corps credibility or damaging relations with our host government.

Often it was still relatively early and nice outside by the time I returned from Estcourt, so I would read, visit with family or neighbors, clean my house, listen to music, or tend to laundry. I had met a young man named Nathi (NOT-ee, short for Nkosinathi, ("God is with us" in Zulu), who lived across the street and was about twenty years old. He spoke flawless English and wanted to become a teacher one day. His older sister, a teacher in Ladysmith, came home most weekends (and probably supported her family financially), as well as keeping an apartment in Ladysmith, shared with another teacher. Nathi was fetching water at the community pump when I met him the first day in my new home. He explained pump etiquette: take turns, defer to elders, help youngsters, and rinse your bucket before filling. Of course, he didn't know I scrubbed my bucket with bleach at least monthly. He was one of the people—along with Mdu and his family—that I didn't get a chance to say a proper good-bye to when I had to leave.

Most nights I went to bed about nine, usually falling asleep to music on an English-speaking Durban radio station that played oldies from the eighties each night, from playlists sent in by listeners. Singers like Whitney Houston, Jim Croce, Karen Carpenter, Anne Murray, Marvin Gaye, Kenny G, Billy Joel, Amy Grant, Elvis Presley and The Eagles. The list would be dedicated to moms, or husbands or significant others. I had just finished putting together my own playlist, to be dedicated to my fellow South African Peace Corps volunteers, when I departed. I had a battery-operated radio in case the power was out. Some nights, if I had power, I played some of my own favorite CDs I'd brought from home. I bought a cheap CD player in Est-court, and left it behind for Spa when I returned to the U.S.

There were a lot of things I might do on a Saturday when I returned from town, but Sundays were more prescribed, especially the afternoons: I almost always went for a walk around the village, taking my camera to photograph kids, animals, birds, people doing interesting things, the beauti-ful views, the only solar power device in Goodhome (there were several in the nearby township of Wembezi). One day I happened upon a group of ten children, boys and girls aged about six to ten or eleven, all swimming naked in the creek while their mothers were napping or doing laundry nearby. When the kids saw that I had a camera they ran up to me and insisted I take pictures, saying, "Shoot me, shoot me!" I did and the next day posted one on Facebook. It resembled one of those pictures I used to see in National Geographic of children in developing countries. It was up for only a few hours when someone must have complained because Facebook took the picture down and sent me an email stating that I had "violated the nudity standard." They warned me not do to it again.

On one Sunday afternoon walk I came upon about twenty-five men in the yard of a home. They insisted I join their circle and one of them found a battered milk crate for me to sit on. I asked the man who had invited me if it was a celebration, an event or a party. "It's a function," he told me, laughing. Soon the Zulu beer was making its way around in a community pitcher. I took a sip and passed it on. Then, goat meat was served—I had noticed a goat hide, dripping blood when I arrived. Before long I was dipping chunks of meat into salt on a traditional wooden tray used for serving goat. Also served was delicious steamed bread, *jeqe*, that accompanies the meat. Before long, many of the men were intoxicated. The men sitting next to me began arguing, poking one another behind my back. *"Time to make my exit,"* I thought. I shook hands or bumped fists with all the men, now about fifty in number (plus ten or so women who were doing all the work), said my "ngiyabongas" and "ngiyajabula ukukukwazes," and escaped. Outside the fence a gaggle of young boys about eight or ten years old—and one girl named Mavis—watched. The group, led by the eleven-year-old Anele (a-NELL-ee), one of my neighbors, escorted me home. *"Gotta start carrying a toothpick in my wallet,"* I said to myself. *"You never know when you'll be invited to a gathering where goat meat is served."* I never did learn what was being celebrated.

After my Sunday afternoon walks I almost always went to the Thuthukani Mazulu, General Dealer store—tuck shop, for short—to buy a loaf of brown bread for my PBJ sandwiches. Occasionally, I would go to the "restaurant" next door, which served two things—meat pies and popcorn, kept hot with a heat lamp like one would find in any American convenience store. It was also the only petrol station for miles. I always took back roads, rather than the main dirt road, not only because it was more interesting, but there was a lot less dust. On one of those walks I met two boys about twelve years old carrying a dead snake about four feet long. I asked if it was a venomous snake. They didn't know. They just knew it had to be killed.

Another afternoon I met a woman who asked me why I was living in Goodhome. She said she'd seen me around many times. I explained about Peace Corps, about Masiphile and our goal of reducing the spread of HIV/ AIDS. She began to cry as she told me her oldest son had died of AIDS the previous year at the age of thirty-one. She thanked me for being in her village. The next day I met a woman about forty who got out of the taxi with me, next to the church. She and her young daughter had clearly done most of the month's shopping in town. She'd called home to ask her teen sons to come help carry the groceries, but there had been no answer. I offered to help and hefted a twenty-five-kilo sack of corn (about fifty-five pounds) onto my shoulder, then picked up my own canvas bag of groceries. She lived nearly a kilometer away, well past Zungu's place. Thankfully, it was downhill and not too hot. She thanked me in Zulu, "Siyabonga," and I was able to respond in Zulu: "Wamukelikhile"—you're welcome. Siyabonga means "we thank you" and is a common alternative to ngiyabonga—"I thank you." When a Zulu speaker says "Siyabonga," even if he is alone, it means he is speaking not only for himself but for all his deceased ancestors who are watching over him.

I often passed small family burial plots, cemeteries really, most of which had probably been there a long time. At Zungu's family compound, his sister—Sendile's mother—was buried right outside my door, the grave covered with a slab of marble and marked with a headstone that read:

"Busisiwe 'Beauty' Zungu, Born 24/01/1962, Died 25/02/2011; Our beloved mother and sister. Rest in peace, Manzini. You will always be loved and remembered." (Note the British way of putting the day before the month: 24/01 is January 24). I never learned the significance of "Manzini," but did discover it is a town in the neighboring country of Swaziland.

I took pictures of it with Sendile's permission. Most families in rural African villages could not afford such displays of wealth. Their deceased loved ones were most likely buried in the backyard, but without nice headstones. Or, the graves might me covered with ordinary rocks, piled up like the ones seen in old Western movies. There were several of those just beyond the fence in the neighbor's yard. Regardless, every family observed the "unveiling," a sacred event one year after death, when the life of the deceased would be celebrated. In true Zulu fashion, relatives, friends and neighbors gather for several hours, usually on a weekend, to tell stories, honor the dead, and partake of much food and home-made beer. There is a similar custom, also called an unveiling, in Jewish culture. It was at one such Zulu event that I ate goat brains, considered a delicacy, for the first time. And at another I ate *inyama yanga phatho*, cow intestines, for the first time. I didn't care for it and after a few bites I discreetly fed the rest to a starving dog. Traditional Zulu dancing and other ancient rites are also often performed at such gatherings. One of my SA25 colleagues, Emily from Alabama, lived for a time with a family that ran the local funeral home out of their attached house. Bodies came and went at all hours of the day and night, sometimes in body bags.

One Friday afternoon, early in my learning curve about Zulu custom, when I had no plans for the weekend, Sendile told me that there would be a "traditional" event that involved slaughtering three goats and serving other food and drink the next day. I was not specifically invited so I didn't join the many people who gathered in the family compound. I stayed in my cinderblock house and read and drank instant coffee, listened to music, worked on a blog entry and played Solitaire on my laptop. About five o'clock Sendile came in and asked if I had gone someplace that day, since he hadn't seen me. I told him I hadn't come because I wasn't invited. He expressed amazement at this, explaining that no invitation was necessary because it's understood in Zulu culture that when someone in the village hosts an event like this, you just show up, especially if you're a man, without being invited. There are certain exceptions, such as a traditional wedding celebration, perhaps, but for most events, no invitation is necessary.

I explained that in the U.S. showing up at a party uninvited is called "crashing." It is frowned on and "usually, no good comes from that since it often means the host runs out of food and drink, people get angry and drunk, neighbors get upset at all the noise and chaos, police are called to break up the annoying party and, often, people end up going to jail for disturbing the peace, resisting arrest, underage drinking or supplying alcohol to a minor. Everybody loses!" It's especially a problem in a college town like the one where I live, I told him. We both had a good laugh and I promised that henceforth I would crash his parties even if I wasn't invited. A few minutes later Hlonie arrived with a big plate of food for me, including the last of the goat brains. That might have been the weekend Sendile brought his two-week old son, Luthanda (a form of the word "love" in Zulu), home for the first time. He was so tiny!

24

Afrikaners: Partiers to Rival Peace Corps Volunteers

Most of the people I met in South Africa were black, of course. Such was the nature of living in a collection of Zulu villages. But I also met memorable whites—in addition to the Coloureds, the Asians and the Indians. Like the U.S., South Africa is a "melting pot." There were many whites in Pretoria: Peace Corps staff, medical people, memorable Peace Corps volunteers other than my SA25 colleagues, soldiers and other Americans from the embassy. And there were Afrikaners from Estcourt.

Peter Buys was a prominent Estcourt businessman and president of the Estcourt Rotary Club. They called him "President Peter." He owned a busy garage and Shell petrol station, the busiest tow service in the area, and a car rental agency. He once told me he was on the lookout for a large piece of property in the area to build a truck stop to add to his collection. I contacted him via email when I wanted to start a clean stove project and needed a local Rotary club as a sponsor. I never formally joined Rotary, but they welcomed me and invited me to special events. When I first contacted Peter he invited me to the next monthly breakfast meeting which was on a Thursday morning at seven at the country club in Estcourt. I could make it only if I caught the first taxi from Goodhome at six a.m. and had a ride from city center to the golf club. He offered to pick me up in front of the post office at 6:45. He did that many times over the next several months so that I could participate in meetings and other activities at least once a month.

It wasn't a very big club. There were never more than ten or twelve people at the breakfast meetings—but it, and Peter, were active and generous. He always insisted on paying for my meal. The club had several worthy projects going on during the time I was involved, including supporting a nearby "orphans and vulnerable children program." That's an official South African government demographic to track the number of children affected by the HIV/AIDS epidemic. At the first meeting Peter introduced me and gave me several minutes to explain about Peace Corps, what I was doing there and why, and about the healthy stove project. My rudimentary math calculations suggested that at least 100,000 early deaths from respiratory illnesses could be prevented over several years, including those of many young children, by bringing cleaner-burning stoves to the area. Most members seemed genuinely interested in the project, asked appropriate questions, and Peter said the board of directors would discuss it and get back to me. It became another project I was unable to pursue because I had to leave Africa early.

I noticed at that first meeting that every member was white. This wasn't surprising since most businesses were owned by whites, who unlike most black people, had the time, energy and resources to participate in something like Rotary. I asked Peter about that and he said they had had black members, specifically a black minister who had been part of the group, but did not have any at that point. I guessed most current members were Afrikaners, though some were probably transplants from England or other Commonwealth countries.

After a couple of months Peter invited me to attend a special evening meeting at the home of members Dave and Arlene, Brits who had moved to South Africa many years before. He said the meeting would be more social than business. Dave and Arlene operated a bed and breakfast, and ran the orphans and vulnerable children program supported by Rotary. Peter had also invited me to spend the night at his home in Mooi River, a small, rural town south of Estcourt.

It turned into a memorable evening. I met Peter at his garage in late afternoon. We drove to his home where I met his attractive and charming wife, Sarah, and his children, teen-agers Brian and Bridget, who gave me a hug. Sarah was a white native of Zimbabwe, one of South Africa's neighbors to the north. I never heard her story, but knew that many white Zimbabweans had fled the country when black President Robert Mugabe came to power in 1987 and instituted land reforms that didn't favor whites. Mugabe is the longest-serving African president and is widely viewed as a dictator. Some of the elections he won allegedly were rigged. South African Peace Corps volunteers are not allowed to travel there, except to go, by air, to Victoria Falls, a popular tourist attraction, because most of the country is not considered safe.

We still had a couple of hours to kill before the dinner, so we traded Peter's late model sedan for his late-eighties Land Rover and went to his favorite biltong shop. Biltong is dried meat similar to jerky that can be made from either domestic or game animals. Afrikaners are proud of their biltong and, I was told, are insulted when Americans call it jerky. It was delicious, and I chose not to test the jerky theory with my new Afrikaner friends. We then went to his favorite watering hole, Argyle House in Mooi River, where we met up with a couple of his friends for a Castle Milk

Stout, a brand of dark beer I had come to like, and rum and Cokes. He introduced me to Brandon, one of his friends, who wore a straw hat that, according to Peter, he never removed. He told me that on a recent night out with the boys, when a woman asked Brandon to take off his hat he told her he wouldn't unless she removed her top. So she did! Everybody laughed, we had another round of drinks, and then left for the tour of Dave and Arlene's OVC program, The Lighthouse, and the braai (BBQ) at their home.

Later, on the drive to Dave and Arlene's, we talked about the South African Police Services. Peter told me about an armed robbery at his business. The employees had called police and officers had responded almost immediately. The robber was still visible, running across a nearby field, and the employees pointed him out to the officers. However, they let him escape, saying they weren't willing to chase someone with a gun.

The steaks were delicious and the alcohol flowed, as did the jokes, mostly by one person, at the expense of Indians and "kaffirs." Kaffir is a derogatory term relating to blacks that is akin to "the N word" in the U.S.; it comes from an Arabic word meaning "infidel." More evidence that some whites are still racist and not accepting of integration. I was also disappointed by white people during a radio call-in show where callers had to answer "slam dunk" trivia questions to win a prize. The question was, "What famous South African turns ninety-five today?" It was Nelson Mandela's birthday, and the radio crew had been talking about it all morning. The caller did not know the answer; nor did her husband, advising her in the background. The DJ gave her a clue: "He's largely responsible for bringing an end to apartheid." The woman's answer? "What's apartheid?" She didn't win the prize.

Peter's wife met us at Dave and Arlene's home, having come in a separate car. Peter explained it was their practice to always take separate cars so that if one of them had a fatal accident, one parent would survive. As we were finishing dinner Peter got a call from a friend who asked to meet him for drinks. Sarah was concerned about how much Peter had already had to drink, but he was nonchalant and off we went again to Argyle House. I figured it was Sarah's idea that they take separate cars. At the bar: more drinks and spirited conversation with a woman named Natalie, about my volunteer work, HIV/AIDS, and South African culture. I don't recall many of the details.

My journal tells me I had four beers and three rum and Cokes over the course of the evening, *the most alcohol I've had in one evening in many decades, maybe ever.* I slept well in Peter's guest house, had a long hot shower in the morning (didn't miss the bucket bath), breakfast with Peter, and returned to Goodhome to find that in my one-night absence someone, probably Hlonie, had mopped the floor and rearranged all the furniture—again.

25

Cooling My Heels in Pretoria and Hanging with SA23

My last two weeks in Africa were bittersweet. I had a great time socializing with Peace Corps volunteers from SA23, who were there for "COS"—close, or completion, of service activities—but I was ending my service, against my will. Some of the 23s were the stuff of legend and though I had met most of them during my fourteen months in South Africa, I would not have gotten to know them so well if not for cooling my heels in Pretoria while the medical people debated my fate. It is Peace Corps policy, Mike, one of the medical officers, told me that when a volunteer gets a new diagnosis during service, the medical staff at HQ in Washington, D.C.—not the medical people in the country of service—decides what happens. I think Mike and Arlene would have let me stay. A year later, as I write these words, my symptoms are no worse than in the beginning, and I think I could have been treated in South Africa. Being a person who looks at both sides of an issue, I understood that the medical staff in Washington could be more objective and had the ability and responsibility to decide what was best for Peace Corps. I should have been a diplomat!

I spent those final two weeks at Khayalethu ("our home" in Zulu), one of several Pretoria backpackers, or hostels, that caters to Peace Corps volunteers. Several were within walking distance of Peace Corps South Africa headquarters, a mile or so away. The brothers who ran it, Scott and DJ, were accommodating and flexible and went out of their way to keep us fed, entertained, and comfortable. At times it was like a mini United Nations. They served low-budget travelers from all over the world, not just Peace Corps volunteers, and all of us met many an interesting person while bunking there. One night an all-black soccer team from out of town partied at a bar after the game and didn't come back to Khayalethu until three a.m., new female friends from the bar in tow. They were loud and were smoking "dagga"— marijuana. Usually, it was quiet at night.

For 150 rand a night, about fifteen dollars, one had a clean, comfortable bed, usually in a room shared with a few others, hot showers, a place to check email, read, visit, watch television, nap, socialize, swim and work on a suntan. They also had the most amazing breakfasts imaginable, including omelets custom-made by DJ, and a bottomless coffee cup. A couple of nights a week one could order pizza, and every Wednesday was trivia night. We formed teams and competed, with the winning team getting a nice bottle of wine or some other prize. One night when a bunch of us from SA25 were in Pretoria for a training event, Niki, Lilly, Emily and a couple of others organized a dinner in honor of an upcoming Jewish holiday, open to all, not just those who were Jewish. We practiced our diversity and the festivities included Lilly and others doing readings in Hebrew.

One person I got to spend time with that weekend was Ethan, a mid-twenties college grad from Rochester, New York, who must be described as charismatic. He was also friendly, sincere, funny, intelligent. I was constantly amazed, and envious, at how he could walk up to any female Peace Corps volunteer in the place and put an arm around her shoulder, give her a hug or come up from behind and give her a surprise neck massage, and she always seemed receptive and pleased at the attention. I could never get away with that! It wouldn't surprise me if one day I read that Ethan had been elected a new senator from New York State, or had become president of a major corporation, or appointed ambassador to a prominent African nation.

One night Ethan led us in singing theme songs from TV shows we could remember—*"Gilligan's Island," " The Beverly Hillbillies," " Davy Crockett," " The Brady Bunch"*—then suggested we reconvene at Livingstone's, a bar not far from the backpacker that had two-for-one drinks during the early evening happy hour. It was a popular gathering place for volunteers in Pretoria, though most of the customers were white. Alyssa from my group was in town for a meeting and joined us. Many of the 23s had completed their COS activities (exit meetings, paperwork, medical and dental exams, turning in project reports and such) and were leaving in the morning. This was the last hurrah. Since I missed COS with my SA25 peers, this time with SA23s was the closest I would come. We all ordered drinks and some of us food. Ethan ordered a "Sowetan Toilet," one for each of us. It was named for the large township, Soweto, outside Johannesburg. The drink included Amarula, banana and chocolate liqueur, and was topped with whipped cream. Tasty.

Sami, a mid-twenties woman from Michigan originally, who was one of our training speakers, told a story about a thirteen-year-old girl in her village girls' group. The girl wanted to know more about "milk sex," a term Sami and the rest of us had never heard. It took much cajoling and coaxing for Sami to get the girl to explain that milk sex is when a woman pours milk over her vagina and allows a cat to lick it off. Apparently, done properly, this produces sexual stimulation. Just when I thought I had learned all I could about the culture. Sami was wearing an African National Congress tee-shirt that night, which would have been a definite no-no the day before when she was still a Peace Corps volunteer.

Also in the group was sixtyish Seth, an attorney from Los Angeles who joined Peace Corps when he burned out from being a partner in a high pressure practice. He was a widower whose wife had died of cancer. He was waiting at Khayalethu for some of his adult children to arrive so they could travel together. Later, he'd visit a son in Germany, maybe go to Australia, and end up driving cross-country in the U.S. to sell his house in LA. Then he'd retire to the Sonoma wine country! I'd met him a few months earlier when he was in Pretoria recovering from knee surgery. He had been stationed in Northwest Province, one of the few Peace Corps South Africa volunteers still there. He had told me a story about a woman in his village who died when her house caught fire and how within hours the house had been stripped of anything of value by other villagers, though he acknowledged they could have been relatives. I guess the house must not have burned completely.

Several people talked about what they did with possessions they didn't want to take back to the U.S., something every volunteer faces. Some said they were made to feel as if their primary contribution to their village was in the stuff they left behind. Sean, my fellow Eugenean, pointed out that Peace Corps staff said there are a variety of ways departing volunteers can deal with this issue. But that they recommend you not set your stuff in a big pile in the front yard and light it on fire, what one volunteer had done a few years earlier. I didn't have much time when it came to making that decision. Ultimately, I made three piles in my little cinderblock house: one for the burn barrel, one for donation to

Masiphile, and one for anyone from the village who wanted something from that pile. I labeled all three shortly before Silence, the Peace Corps driver, arrived to transport me back to Pretoria for the long flight home.

A volunteer I'd never met before, Andy, told us about his dog, a village mutt that had belonged to a neighbor, who often abused the animal. One day the dog escaped and ran to Andy's place. He kept it, cared for it, fed it properly. After a month the abusive neighbor knocked on the door and demanded the dog's return. Andy refused to give it up. The next day the neighbor liberated the dog when Andy was gone and held it for ransom. Negotiations ensued and ultimately Andy paid 1,200 rand (about $120) for the return of his pet. What in America would be animal abuse, burglary and extortion was just the cost of doing neighborly business in a rural village. Another departing SA23er, Melissa, was spending 5,000 rand, about $500, to take her three-legged village mutt, Brook, home to America.

Also in the group that night was early-thirties Oklahoman Roy, a guitar-playing folk singer who wrote a lot of his own material. A very talented man, I watched him play and sing several times. Roy was tall and thin and wore his long brown hair in a ponytail. He had worked as a care provider for disabled people before joining Peace Corps. Though younger, he bore a striking resemblance to Fabio Lanzoni, the famous Italian actor and model best known for his appearances on romance paperback novel covers in the 1980s and '90s. Roy and I didn't talk much that night at Livingstone's—too loud—but, after the party, I was laying on my bed back at Khayalethu and I heard Roy playing softly outside on the patio. I couldn't sleep so I joined him. That's when he told me he'd been mistaken for Fabio when, at a Pretoria mall, he had been standing near a poster with the real Fabio's picture on it, modeling sportswear. He also told me his father, a newspaper editor, had read one of my posts on Facebook where I described Roy singing one night at Khayalethu. I laughed and told Roy, "I never cease to be amazed at the obscure, to me, people who read me on FB or my blog." Once, early in service, I heard from the adult children of Vivian, our senior colleague, who told me they had been trolling the Internet for information about Peace Corps in South Africa and came across the blog entry in which I talked about their mother. They were surprised and pleased.

Roy also told me one of the most amazing Peace Corps volunteer stories I'd heard in Africa. When I knew him he was posted to a village in Limpopo. But, he told me, he'd been originally placed with an organization in Loskop, near where I and Kristin, also from SA25, were living in KZN. But after a few months Roy was moved for his protection. His host family's father had been shot in a local political power struggle over who would become village chief, not an unusual occurrence in rural villages. (The man had a prosthetic leg, the result of an earlier shooting). The man's car was peppered with twenty shots, three of which hit him, in the face, arm and leg. He survived and later he and Roy attended a wedding in nearby Bergville. They both had too much to drink, Roy said, and that night, driving home, the man asked Roy to protect his family if anything should happen to him. Roy agreed because he was drunk. The man then handed Roy his gun and Roy made a foolish, alcohol-inspired promise that he would shoot the man's enemy if he saw him. They even drove by one of the local taverns that night looking for the target, but, thankfully, they didn't find him. When Roy sobered up he reported his adventure to Peace Corps, and was promptly moved to a new village hundreds of miles away. Earlier at Khayalethu I heard the story of Janell, a young woman from New Jersey, an SA24 education volunteer, who told me she was evacuated from her village because her school had been burned down in a local dispute over a tar road not being extended to the school. She was hanging out in Pretoria while Peace Corps decided if it was safe for her to return.

Many departing 23s had big plans for when their Peace Corps service concluded: travel, starting or looking for work, grad school. Roy had no plans except for a music gig at a coffee house in his home town of Norman, Oklahoma. Wish I could have been there.

Toward the end of my last stay in Pretoria I got to spend some time with Julie—my fellow leftie—who was in her second placement in Limpopo, having been relocated from her initial post, for safety reasons. Like Ethan, she was from Rochester, New York. We were pretty close during training and I had nominated her to be one of SA25's representatives on the Volunteer Advisory Council that interacted with Peace Corps South Africa management. But she was far away in Limpopo and I didn't see her for months at a time, though we did communicate via text, phone or email. She had come from Polokwane, a large city in Limpopo, on the hospital shuttle van that brought people to Pretoria for medical appointments. She called it "the love bus" and described many of the colorful people she had ridden with for hours: psychiatric patients, people in their pajamas, people who could barely walk, and people critically ill who in the U.S. would likely be transported by ambulance. She loved being a world traveler and bettering the planet. I expected she would follow her passion and end up doing international humanitarian work in a different country, perhaps elsewhere in Africa, after a visit home.

He wasn't with me in Pretoria for my last two weeks as a Peace Corps volunteer, but I can't write a book about my experience without honoring Greg Mork, my friend and fellow SA25er. I became friends with Greg and his wife Pat, one of our two married couples from Seattle, in part because we were peers, all of us sixtyish. More significantly, Greg was an inspiration. Originally, he was from a small town in North Dakota (one of only three states I've never been to), but had been a contractor in Seattle for a few decades. His specialty was roofing, but he could build or fix just about anything—and he could kill venomous snakes (see Chapter 5).

On the final day of training—while the rest of us were fretting about last-minute packing, saying good-bye to friends and wondering about our new placements—Greg was worried about a new septic system he had been working on for weeks, a project at the home of his host family. Earlier he built them a sturdy ladder from a couple of tree poles and scrap lumber. Like many older volunteers, Greg had resources that could be tapped if needed, unlike volunteers just out of college who didn't have much work history, let alone a pension or investments. Whenever we would meet in Pretoria or other places Greg would tell me about his latest project. He had planted a big garden, fixed broken windows or a leaking roof, done plumbing repairs, refurbished broken furniture, put in irrigation pipes for watering and had fixed a dilapidated well. All out of his own cookie jar. He always wanted to stop at hardware stores and lumber yards to look for a tool, or a certain screw or nail or an adhesive. His organization was small and sometimes didn't have a lot for him to do, so he would develop his own projects, not all of them involving building or fixing things. Many of us dealt with that issue at times and had to be creative, but most of us didn't possess Greg's skills or his toolbox.

He coached a boys' soccer team called "The MMC Boys" (for medical male circumcision) and used the team name to start conversations to encourage men and teen-agers to consider the procedure. He also had a unique way of dealing with panhandlers: He carried a bag of oranges wherever he went and when people asked him for money for food he offered them an orange. A few months after my return I got an email from Pat, thanking me for a donation I had made to one of her projects. She wrote about Greg's latest endeavor: "Greg is building a house for a gogo with twelve grandchildren to look after, to replace their falling down one-room hut. He has gathered some salvaged materials but otherwise is financing it out of pocket." No surprise there. I'd guess that many of those twelve children were orphans or otherwise vulnerable. I'm proud of my Peace Corps endeavors, as I imagine most of my fellow 25ers are—despite the frustrations we encountered. But how many—the thirty-six original members of SA25 or those other 215,000 Peace Corps volunteers who have served in the fifty-three years of Peace Corps existence—can say they more-or-less single-handedly built a house for a grandmother and twelve homeless grandkids? Greg and I used to get mixed up once in a while, especially in the beginning, because we were about the same age, had white hair and four-letter names that started with "g" and had an "r" in the middle. I would say that I didn't mind being mistaken for Greg because he was good lookin' and a great guy.

Greg and Pat also had the experience that many volunteers, though not me, had when someone they knew personally died. A woman from their organization near Greytown, KZN, and a friend, had been killed when their car crashed into a bridge abutment. It was at night and speculation was that he was tired and fell asleep at the wheel. South African irony. Greg and Pat attended the funeral. They also told of an 18-year-old who had been raped by her father when she was younger, but had come forward to seek safety and speak about her experience; and about a fourteen-year-old boy who had to be carried into their organization's office because he was so weak from the effects of late-stage AIDS. His grandmother had administered his anti-retroviral medication, but had become confused and stopped them. The boy died.

On another occasion an SA26 volunteer, Oregonian Connie, reported that a newborn baby was abandoned in her village. People named it Nelson and hoped someone would adopt him. Another volunteer, an older education volunteer from an earlier group, Tom, wrote a sad and poignant first-person account for the Peace Corps South Africa newsletter about being present when one of his students, a six-year-old boy, was struck by a car and killed. I had met Tom, who was about my age, a couple of months earlier when we shared a room at Khayalethu. He had just returned from a long visit to the states, before extending his two-year commitment by a year, an option that a few volunteers from each group usually do. He didn't think he had accomplished all that he could. He proudly showed me a big suitcase full of pencils, paper, pens and other supplies he had collected for his school while home. I'm sure his thoughts when he decided to extend didn't include the possibility that he would hold the hand of a dying child.

All of these things, and others, also happen in America: abandoned babies, children hit by cars, people who die of AIDS, fatal car crashes, people who die of snake bites or lightning strikes or are killed by violent domestic partners. But in the U.S. they aren't nearly as routine as they are in developing, largely rural, African countries.

26

Reflections

When I completed my Community Needs Assessment early
in my placement at Masiphile, the document to help me decide my projects for the next two years, I identified sixteen
possibilities. Ultimately, in consultation with Nonhlanhla,
we narrowed it to nine: expand the big garden, build a website, start GrassRoots Soccer and life skill programs at the
school, develop an income-generating project or two (sell
products handmade by the gogos, chickens and eggs, and
recyclables), the cleaner burning stove project, help with
Operation Sakuma Sahke, and write a grant to build a playground for the Masiphile créche.

The grant to buy and install playground equipment for
the kids would have been funded partly by the Peace Corps
Partnership Program, which called for the African community to contribute labor, land and materials equal to at least
twenty-five percent of the total cost. The rest would have
come from PCPP funds, including donations from my local
returned Peace Corps volunteer organization, West Cascade
back in Eugene, with whom I had kept in touch. One of its
primary missions is to raise funds to support projects of Oregon volunteers. I wrote the grant proposal, which had been
positively reviewed by the Peace Corps South Africa grants
coordinator, with some minor changes, and the playground
equipment identified from a supplier in Durban. That I was

unable to complete this project was one of my biggest disappointments when I was sent home. I tried to get another volunteer to pick up the ball and take it the final few yards for a touchdown, but that wasn't possible.

The projects that were clearly successful included the garden expansion, the website and, to some extent, the project that enabled the gogos to sell their products to buyers in the U.S. Unfortunately, I was unable to get an on-going process in place before I left. The one-time-only projects—getting a donor to buy us a printer and designing and building the nice sign for Masiphile—were successful. I provided support to Operation Sakuma Sahke, the ambitious program that identifies people in Imbabazane with serious social needs. Other projects didn't get off the ground for a variety of reasons.

On February 21, 2013, a month before I learned I would not be completing my second year, I was, nonetheless, thinking about my projects, my successes, and lack of success with some of them. In my journal that night I wrote:

A modest playground doesn't seem like much of an accomplishment for two years of effort. (Earlier I had described it as the "capstone" of my service). *I see Masiphile as a pretty unsophisticated organization. We have virtually no money— only the modest crèche fees and now some food from the Department of Agriculture—but everyone is a volunteer except the crèche teachers, who can't possibly get what they deserve. Everyone else, including Nonhlanhla, works for free. Every day is a struggle. I vacillate daily between whether the state of this modest, poorly-funded operation is reason enough for me to have accomplished so little, or is that just a rationalization on my part for why I've not accomplished much compared to what I thought I would do, and what some of my fellow SA25ers have achieved.*

How do I judge the small, but important, daily interactions and events that contributed to the big picture: learning about Zulu culture, educating South Africans about the U.S; remembering the HIV positive young man I counseled; the teen-agers I talked to about condom use; the hundreds if not thousands of meaningful interactions with people of all stripes, all over South Africa; the countless friends I made in many villages; the influence I may have had on dozens of Masiphile volunteers I mingled with frequently; relationships with Mdu and Amanda and their family, and Nonhlanhla and her relatives. I will cherish my friendship with Zungu and his kin. I'll never forget the old man who needed a pair of shoes; the many books I donated to the library; Maria in Bundu and the reading glasses I gave her; the sharing of Zulu beer, goat brains and piles of pap at family gatherings I was graciously invited to, and at which I proudly represented America. What about the help and support I gave to Sindisiwe and her family, which had nothing directly to do with my assignment, but was important to them and to me? In the end I'd like to think these things were as important as the assignment, perhaps even more so.

And what about the other volunteers—Linda, Greg and Pat, Julie, Rachel, Linda, Peggie, Vivian, Alyssa, Ann, Theresa, Lilly, Dan and the rest? Some of these could turn into life-long friendships, which would certainly benefit me, if not Africa.

The day that I finished writing this book I came across a website, skollworldforum.org, that included a list of "25 Tips for Peace Corps Volunteers," suggested by Kathy Gau, who was a Peace Corps volunteer many years ago. All were good tips, but the ones that resonated with me were:

"You will not see tangible, measurable results in two years anywhere close to what you hope or expect. The saying that 'what takes a day in USA takes a week in Africa, what takes a week in USA takes a month in Africa, what takes a month in USA takes one year in Africa' is close to true for reasons over which you have no control. So after your first month on the job, when you are still in USA mode, write down what you would like to achieve in two months' time. This now becomes your two-year work goal.

"There is no 'us and them.' Human beings are the same everywhere. Could you do it if it were you in their shoes? Don't think for a moment that because you live in a hut and don't make much money that you are in their shoes. In your life in the USA, how much of your achievements to date really reflect on you? Or did you just make good use of the opportunities provided you? For certain you did not need to build the systems, government and schools associated with creating these opportunities. Perhaps your great grandparents did, but not you."

Years before I joined Peace Corps I had heard about volunteers who said they got more out of their time in Peace Corps than they contributed to their villages or countries of service. It's become almost a cliché that so many volunteers describe their experiences in such terms. There are now hundreds of thousands of former volunteers, most of whom probably had positive experiences. Many are U.S. diplomats or elected officials—U.S. ambassador to Libya, Christopher Stevens, killed in an attack on the consulate in Benghazi in September 2012, was a Peace Corps volunteer in Morocco, 1983-85. Others are leaders in business or communication, or work in international health or development programs, education or other positions of influence where they can show others that there may be paths that avoid or lessen conflict, that promote peace or resolution. These are people who adopted positive ways of dealing with others, and who have been influenced by their two years in a place vastly different from their homes in the states. Their experiences have shown them that people, at their most basic level, are more-or-less the same everywhere. And the people who live in those villages, towns and cities? They will see the same is true of average Americans.

Change is inevitable, and that applies to Peace Corps. In the February 26, 2013 issue of the "Yale Journal of International Affairs" Christopher Hedrick, country director in Senegal 2007-2012 and, in 2013, Coordinator of Special Initiatives for Peace Corps Africa Region, wrote about the "New Peace Corps," not to be confused with, "The image of the solitary Peace Corps volunteer, an icon of 'Peace Corps Classic,' "as Sargent Shriver, the agency's first director, constructed it in the 1960s," Hedrick said. "While the Peace Corps evolved over the decades, much remained unchanged. Volunteers served in relative isolation, with few opportunities for outside communication and collaboration. They integrated into their host communities with deep linguistic and cultural understanding. Their development impact was largely evaluated anecdotally.

"This new approach redefines the Peace Corps development niche, taking advantage of the new generation of volunteers and of technology. 'Millennials' are tech savvy and want frequent communication and feedback. They have grown up working in teams. They're goal-oriented and seek a sense of accomplishment and recognition. This new generation of volunteers is entering service as access to technology is dramatically expanding in the developing world. Cell phone penetration in some countries in Africa now surpasses the United States, and Internet access is growing exponentially around the world.

"In the New Peace Corps, mobile devices are used to access free, universally accessible technology platforms…(and) teamwork is replacing the iconic notion of the lone volunteer. Increasingly, volunteers are collaborating to pursue bold goals and teaming up with partners, such as international NGOs and USAID, to work for important change," Hedrick concluded.

This was happening in South Africa when I served and will continue to happen all over the world. Peace Corps and the "new" volunteers should continue to embrace such change in the interest of Peace Corps volunteers maximizing their effectiveness, but also should never forget the value of developing the very human one-to-one connections that are the hallmark of Peace Corps service. A Peace Corps recruiter in Eugene told me that the organization is adopting policies that will enable volunteers to have a greater say in which country they serve, provided they have the necessary skills. This can only increase the number of qualified people who may consider Peace Corps service.

Peace Corps has improved in other important ways: In recent years it has embraced changes in safety and security policies and procedures, in ways that make it more sensitive and responsive to incidents of violence against volunteers. The Kate Puzey Peace Corps Volunteer Protection Act of 2011 is an example. It was enacted after the twenty-four-year-old Kate, from Atlanta, Georgia, was murdered in West Africa in 2009. Peace Corps also has improved its response to sexual assault incidents in the past couple of years. I saw evidence of this in South Africa. Critics say there is still room for improvement.

In 2001, Ohio Democratic Representative Dennis Kucinich, who later ran for president (I voted for him), introduced legislation to form a cabinet-level Department of Peace. His was just the latest in a long line of legislators who, over many decades, have done the same. Others have done so since. Perhaps it's time to revisit that idea—and actually do it. The "New Peace Corps" can lead the way.

27

A Tribute to Nelson Mandela,
a Hero for the Ages

When I left for South Africa in January 2012 to be a Peace Corps volunteer my mission was to help reduce the spread of HIV/AIDS in the country with the world's highest rate. Had someone asked me what my second goal was, I might have said, "To meet Nelson Mandela." I never achieved that goal before I returned home in late March of 2013.

Mandela's death at ninety-five in December 2013 meant I never will meet him, nor will millions of black South Africans whose lives were changed forever when, in 1994, he became the first democratically elected black president of the country, ending a history that existed for hundreds of years. He became president not long after he was released from prison, after twenty-seven years, for political activism.

Madeleine Albright, President Bill Clinton's Secretary of State, wrote in her autobiography that meeting Mandela was like "having George Washington introduce himself." As a United Nations ambassador, Albright described Mandela as "the globe's most famous and respected man. He was the embodiment of his nation's liberation from apartheid and a leader who taught the world a profound lesson about choosing reconciliation." There are lessons for all in that philosophy.

Mandela was hospitalized frequently during the time I lived in a Zulu village, a couple hundred miles from where he grew up. Some of his health problems were typical for an elderly man, but many were the result of respiratory problems related to tuberculosis he contracted when he was imprisoned. When he was hospitalized in December 2012, I posted on Facebook: "People here are nervous when Mandela is hospitalized. He's an icon of freedom and democracy after imprisonment and hundreds of years of domination of black South Africans by whites. I'm amazed when I think how, under Mandela, a civil war that could have claimed millions was avoided. He's a hero in every sense." I cried when I wrote those words, as I cried upon learning of his death.

It's impossible for me to describe how black South Africans feel about Mandela, often called Madiba, his clan name. During one of his hospitalizations, a Soweto Township resident was quoted, "We need him very, very much. But what can we do? If God calls, it's time, because he's old now." Not long before, Mandela was honored by having his picture on all five denominations of the South African currency.

I wasn't there to share sorrow with my African friends, but I know there were many tears. People were devastated, and many likely wondered if South Africa could pursue Madiba's dream without his guidance and his living presence. But there was also much celebration—of his life, of his accomplishments, his love for his people. Black South Africans, especially Zulus, love a good party and there was plenty of celebration in honor of "Tata"—"father" in Xhosa, one of the many tribal languages. There are white South Africans who not only didn't lament Mandela's passing, but, rather, mourn loss of white rule. Many white South Africans fled the country rather than live under government with a black ruler. But there are also many whites who admired, respected and supported Mandela.

Many problems continue under the African National Congress—the ruling party that has governed since the beginning of democracy. These include one of the highest crime rates on earth, poverty, corruption and violence, including a high rate of sexual assault. But Mandela's legacy is secure, and should be, though he made only a dent in these problems. It will take years to address them, and generations to eliminate the internalized oppression that has been 500 years in the making.

Mandela described himself as "fundamentally an optimist. Whether that comes from nature or nurture, I cannot say. Part of being optimistic is keeping one's head pointed toward the sun, one's feet moving forward. There were many dark moments when faith in humanity was tested, but I would not, could not give myself up to despair. That way lays defeat and death…"

It would be good to remember other of his words. "No one is born hating another person because of the color of his skin, or his background, or religion," Mandela said. "People learn to hate, and if they can learn to hate, they can be taught to love, for love comes more naturally to the human heart."

That's the Mandela philosophy we should emulate.

My Peace Corps service in South Africa, despite its abbreviated course, was one of the signature events of my life. It would not have been possible without Nelson Mandela and others, such as President Kennedy, who envisioned a world that focuses on living in peace and helping one another, rather than on ruling or subjugating others who have different values, cultures or beliefs.

Long before we arrived in South Africa and began pre-service training (PST) we learned about Peace Corps' three goals:

"To help the people of interested countries in meeting their need for trained men and women; to help promote a better understanding of Americans on the part of the peoples served; and to help promote a better understanding of other peoples on the part of Americans."

Now that I've done all that I can to help achieve the first two goals—served as a Peace Corps Volunteer in South Africa and represented U.S. culture and values to South African citizens—all that remains is for me to practice the "Third Goal," teaching Americans about South Africans. I hope this book will help accomplish that. Peace Corps devotes a lot of resources to pursuing that goal and I expect that, for the rest of my life, I will endeavor to assist in the effort. I hope my fellow SA25ers and all Peace Corps volunteers everywhere, current and returned, will do the same.

While I was in Africa I read that Peace Corps' entire budget for its first fifty years was an amount equal to what the U.S. government spends on its military/defense every five days. I read recently that we've spent about $5 trillion on the wars in Iraq and Afghanistan. Imagine what could have been accomplished if we had spent half that much on pursuing peace.

A shorter version of this chapter appeared as an op-ed in the Eugene Register Guard, December 8, 2013

Epilogue

Sindisiwe: I was unable to arrange for Sindisiwe to come to the U.S. for a visit. The barriers were insurmountable. In late 2013 I wrote her a letter that said, in part, "Read these next few lines carefully because they are the most important lines in this letter:

"You deserve to be with a man who treats you with respect, who honors and treasures you for the wonderful person you are. You are beautiful, intelligent, kind, funny, a good mother, a good daughter and granddaughter, a hard worker. You have good values and beliefs. You deserve—and your boys deserve—a man who will be a good role model for them, who will never abuse you, physically or emotionally, who does not abuse drugs or alcohol, who will work with you to provide for your family. A man who accepts that your goals and dreams are just as important as his, and who helps you reach them. Please don't settle for, don't accept, anything less. You deserve the best. It will not be easy to find such a man, but you must never give up, never accept anything less than what you deserve. You are a young woman and have many years ahead of you, and should spend them with a man deserving of you. Any man would be so lucky to be with you."

I sent the letter to the primary school in her village, since I had no other address. In January 2014 I called her on her birthday and she confirmed that she had received it. We had a bittersweet conversation that nonetheless ended on a positive note.

Rachel: I told much of the most memorable parts of Rachel's story in the book, but not the final episode. I share it now with her blessing. She received much support from Peace Corps and others after the traumatic episode in Bergville, KZN, her initial placement, where she was accosted by a large group of intoxicated men who harassed and touched her mercilessly. Earlier, she missed a big chunk of PST because she was ill, and later she fell and broke an ankle. Eventually, this SA25er was placed with an organization called Bhekuzulu Self Sufficient Project, just a few miles from me, making her even closer to me than Kristin. Rachel had been there a short time when a man held a knife to her throat and demanded five rand. She was in a colleague's car at the time and the man was an acquaintance of the colleague and claimed he was joking. I suspect Rachel experienced some of the same reactions as before, which is common with Post Traumatic Stress Disorder (PTSD). Not long after that Rachel learned that her grandmother, to whom she was very close, was quite ill. Rachel made the decision to return home, but her grandmother died while Rachel was flying over the Atlantic Ocean. Once home she decided not to return to Africa, in part so she could support her grandfather. Rachel found a satisfying job working for People for the Ethical Treatment of Animals (PETA), and is doing well. If there were a Peace Corps award for gumption and never giving up in the face of adversity, Rachel would have won it—hands down!

Lilly: This mid-twenties SA25 colleague from San Francisco—who said she would throw herself in front of a mamba for me—found love in Peace Corps, in the form of Alan, from SA24. She invited us to their wedding, scheduled for August 2014.

Julie: This SA25er, whom I wrote about in one of the last chapters, was described this way: "She loved being a world traveler and bettering the planet. I expected she would follow her passion and end up doing international humanitarian work in a different country, perhaps elsewhere in Africa." Shortly after I wrote those words she posted this note on Facebook: "After twenty-seven months in South Africa supporting maternal and newborn care initiatives, I will be moving to Sierra Leone in May to continue the pursuit of saving mothers giving life."

John Jacoby: Country Director John Jacoby was diagnosed with pancreatic cancer a few months after I left early. He experienced the same fate I did—early discharge from Peace Corps for medical reasons—including finding himself winging his way home within twenty-four hours. At last report his treatment was going well. He was replaced by Julie Burns, who had been country director in the West African Republic of Guinea.

Paige and Dan: These two SA25ers extended their service by a year, convincing Peace Corps they had more to accomplish in their villages, Paige in the same area as where Sindisiwe lives, and Dan in the KZN town of Empangeni.

Me: My symptoms of Parkinson's are no worse now than they were when I was first diagnosed in Pretoria. I've joined a support group, but, because my symptoms are minor, have not taken medication. I work part time off and on, do a lot of volunteer work, and have appeared in two public service announcements on local television in support of recycling. I'm thinking about calling Michael J. Fox to ask him if he wants to do a PSA on Parkinson's with me! I follow the news in South Africa and am active in my local returned Peace Corps volunteer organization, especially in "Third Goal" activities.

I will continue to travel and learn about other cultures. I will never be embarrassed by security inspectors in airports seeing the condoms—alongside shampoo, toothpaste, and soap—in my large see-through baggies on the conveyor belt. Because I'm a Peace Corps volunteer, always will be, and I know the importance of setting a good example and sharing the accoutrements of safe sex with those who really need them.

Gary Cornelius, Eugene, OR, USA/June 2014

13404417R00160

Made in the USA
San Bernardino, CA
21 July 2014